LET ME ENTERTAIN YOU

State Library OF Ohio

SEO Library Center
40780 SR 821 * Caldwell, OH 43724

LET ME ENTERTAIN YOU

Conversations with Show People

by Jordan R. Young

Moonstone Press

To Mickey Katz and Jester Hairston
Brothers under the skin

LET ME ENTERTAIN YOU
Conversations With Show People

FIRST EDITION
Published by Moonstone Press, P.O. Box 142, Beverly Hills CA 90213

Several of the chapters in this book previously appeared in different formats in *The Los Angeles Times, The New York Times, The Christian Science Monitor* and *The Los Angeles Herald-Examiner*. Alternate versions of the chapters on Doodles Weaver and George Rock first appeared in *Spike Jones and his City Slickers*, copyright © 1984 by Jordan R. Young.

Copyright © 1988 by Jordan R. Young

Printed in the United States of America

Cover design by Jack Ritchard
Typeset by Suzette Mahr, Words & Deeds, Los Angeles, California

Library of Congress Cataloging in Publication Data

Young, Jordan R.
    Let me entertain you.

    Bibliography:p.
    Includes index.
    1. Entertainers—Interviews.   I. Title.
PN1583.Y68   1988   790.2'092'2   88-9152
ISBN 0-940410-83-4 (pbk. : alk. paper)

The paper used in this publication meets the minimum requirements of American National Standards for Information Sciences, Permanance of Paper for Printed Library Materials ANSI Z39.48-1984

10 9 8 7 6 5 4 3 2 1

Contents

Foreword

Several years ago, my wife and I were invited to a Christmas party in Hollywood where, it turned out, the only person we knew was the host. We felt a bit lost, trying to mingle, when suddenly Alice tugged my sleeve. "Look," she said, motioning to a man sitting at the bar. "It's Huntz Hall."

Huntz Hall! The evening was an automatic success. We sidled up alongside him, introduced ourselves, and engaged him in conversation. It didn't take long to realize that this man, who was permanently imbedded in our minds as that Dead End kid, was quite a different person in real life: a fifty-year veteran of show business who prided himself on his work in the theater, and the fact that he continued to work on the stage. It was a treat to listen to him, and we felt slightly embarrassed that we'd both fallen into the trap of thinking that the actor would turn out to be just like the role he played so well (perhaps *too* well) in all those Bowery Boys movies.

Jordan Young didn't meet Huntz Hall by accident; he sought him out, to get his story down on paper. Everyone in show business has a story to tell, and if you're a show-biz buff like me, you often find the most interesting storytellers to be the ones who *aren't* the most celebrated. I must confess that when I read the list of subjects in this book, I nodded respectfully at the names of Jack Nicholson and Peter Sellers... but I chortled with glee at the inclusion of Doodles Weaver, Mickey Katz and lovely Laura La Plante. Jordan cared enough to find them and persuade them to talk.

I'm so glad he did. I didn't get to meet Clyde Cook or Reginald Owen when they were alive, but thanks to Jordan, at least I can get to know them a little bit, vicariously. And if, at the same time, I can get some interesting new insights from contemporary actors like Jack Lemmon and Donald Sutherland, well, let's just call that the icing on the cake.

Leonard Maltin

About the Author

Jordan R. Young is a freelance writer-photographer whose work has appeared in *The Los Angeles Times, The New York Times, The Christian Science Monitor, The People's Almanac* and other publications. He is the author of several books, including *Spike Jones and his City Slickers, Reel Characters: Great Movie Character Actors, The Beckett Actor* and the forthcoming *Acting Solo: The Art of One-Man Shows*. He is co-author of the new one-character play, *An Evening with Edna St. Vincent Millay*.

Preface

June 26, 1979. It is a day like any other day on which a comedian might be turned loose in a monastery... a day like any other day in Hollywood.

Marty Feldman is in the midst of setting up a surrealistic sight gag on Stage 34 at Universal Studios. The mock monk huddles with the crew, discussing the placement of the camera. On the wall of the monastery set is a mural of the Last Supper, which looks almost too normal from a distance. On closer inspection Judas bears more than a passing resemblance to Sammy Davis Jr. Beneath a fold-out table, the feet of Jesus and the Apostles are soaking in tubs of water. There is a shark fin protruding from one of the tubs.

Feldman is wearing a straw hat, a Famous Amos T-shirt, blue jeans and sandals. The publicist introduces me at a break in the shooting. I'm there "to observe," she tells the cockeyed, frizzy-haired comic. "Fine, fine," he says, in a gentle English accent. "Look around." He presents me with his left profile, his back and his right profile, then turns to face me. He pulls up his T-shirt to display his belly. "If you don't see what you want," he says earnestly, "just ask for it."

Show people are an accommodating breed of humankind, although not all members of the entertainment industry I've met over the past two decades have been as obliging as the late Marty Feldman. The artificial monastery would have been an appropriate setting for an interview — for what is an interview but a confessional? — but, regrettably, we only had time for a brief chat.

It is not the glitz and glamour of show business that has always intrigued me, nor the setting; the lifestyles of the rich and famous are *their* business. I'm far more interested in what lies behind the facade — how do they do what they do, and why? How do they feel about what they do? What drives them to emote, to perform, to entertain?

The cast of *Let Me Entertain You* is an eclectic one that draws its players from a wide variety of show business experiences, from the English music hall to the Broadway stage, from the silent movie era to the contemporary cinema. The voices in these pages belong to yesterday's personalities as well as today's, both the celebrated and the obscure.

Several of the entertainers whose reminiscences appear in this volume are deceased or long retired. Home video and cable TV have brought some of them back to life. Others are forgotten; their work has vanished.

But because they are no longer in the public eye does not make them any less important. I feel it is all the more reason to include them in these pages, especially if they have passed away.

The entertainment business has taken on a new perspective in recent years, with the blitz of media coverage at every turn — the media itself treading a fine line between journalism and voyeurism — and the incessant awards programs televised to an ever-increasing public. But it should perhaps be noted that it was not always the glamorous and respectable field of endeavor it has become today.

"Anybody in show biz or music or anything, that was about as low as you could get," observes trumpeter George Rock, who gained fame in the 1940s as one of Spike Jones' City Slickers. "We were a pretty low form of life."

I wish to thank the following people for their assistance on this project: Dick Bann, Elliot Chang, Tony Chiu, Suzy Dunster, Marge Hairston, Mike Hawks, Ted Hering, Ronnie James, Ruth Johnson, Grace Katz, Garrett Lee, Frank Liberman, Leonard Maltin, Michael Maslansky, Carolyn Matthews, Dan Pasternack, Eileen Peterson, Douglas Reid, Randy Skretvedt, David Steinberg, Connie Stewart, Edna Tromans, Pam Young, Philip and Pearl Young.

Thanks are due also to: Academy of Motion Picture Arts and Sciences; Alladin Books; Allied Artists; American International; Avco Embassy; Eddie Brandt's Saturday Matinee; Capital Cities/ABC; Alan Bunce, *The Christian Science Monitor*; Claremont College; Columbia Broadcasting System; Columbia Pictures; Culver City Studios; Larry Edmunds Bookshop; Goldwyn Pictures; Harvey Levine, Harlequin Dinner Theatre; Huntington Hartford Theatre; Jalem Productions; Lorimar Productions; *The Los Angeles Herald Examiner*; Connie Koenenn and Irv Letofsky, *The Los Angeles Times*; Mayfair Music Hall; Metro-Goldwyn-Mayer; *The New York Times*; Paramount Pictures; RKO Radio Pictures; Hal Roach Studios; *The San Diego Tribune*; Shubert Theatre; Sons of the Desert; 20th Century-Fox; Universal Pictures; United Artists.

Finally, I am much indebted to the subects themselves, without whose candor and amiable cooperation there would have been no book.

Jordan R. Young
Los Angeles
1988

IN AND OUT OF CHARACTER

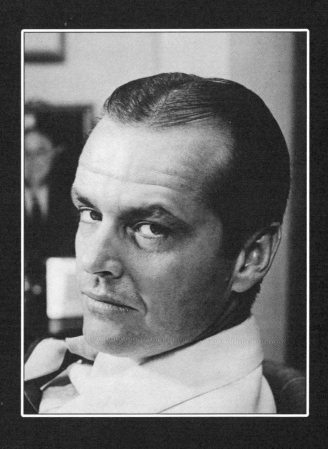

Jack Nicholson

After years of low-budget exploitation movies, Jack Nicholson established
himself on the Hollywood scene with a series of virtuoso portrayals of
soul-searching individuals, prompting The New York Times *to label*
him — to his annoyance — "the reigning anti-hero of American films."
He has been working to destroy the image ever since; in recent years,
many of his characterizations have taken on a self-mocking tone.

Nicholson made his debut on April 22, 1936 in Neptune, New Jer-
sey, to parents who separated before he was born. Being "part of a genera-
tion raised on cool jazz and Jack Kerouac" — and an abundance of mov-
ies — the budding existentialist went "on the road" himself following
high school graduation, and traveled to Los Angeles.

He started as an office boy at MGM in 1954, "a combination of car-
toon department and mailroom." He then studied acting at the Players
Ring Theatre and soon became a regular on popular daytime TV shows
like Divorce Court *and* Matinee Theatre; *he graduated to feature films*
with The Cry Baby Killer *(1958), which was produced by Roger Cor-*
man.

Nicholson made some 20 pictures in the decade that followed,
including several for Corman. Among his early efforts were the original
The Little Shop of Horrors *(in which he played the masochist in the*
dentist's chair), a pair of existential westerns he co-produced with
*director Monte Hellman (*The Shooting *and* Ride in the Whirlwind,
which he also wrote) and The Monkees' Head, *which he co-wrote and co-*
produced with director Bob Rafelson.

His performance as a young lawyer who drops out of his middle-
class existence and takes to the road on a motorcycle, in Easy Rider
(1969), won him an Oscar nomination for Best Supporting Actor and
quickly made him in demand. Among the memorable portrayals that

With Carolyn Mitchell in his film debut, *The Cry Baby Killer* (1958).

With then-wife Sandra Knight in Roger Corman's *The Terror* (1963).

followed were that of a pianist-turned-oil rigger in Five Easy Pieces *and a repressed radio monologist in* The King of Marvin Gardens, *both directed by Rafelson; a brutal womanizer in* Carnal Knowledge; *the worldly navy man in Hal Ashby's* The Last Detail; *and the cynical detective in Roman Polanski's* Chinatown.

Nicholson was riding the crest of a wave in 1974 with Chinatown *when he granted an interview at Culver City Studios in Los Angeles, between takes of* The Fortune. *"I've had a series of pretty good reviews now for some years, and I'm just kind of waiting for the axe to fall," the actor observed. The remark was strangely prophetic: two years later, his career went into a tailspin after his Academy Award-winning perform-ance as the charismatic misfit, Randle P. McMurphy, in* One Flew Over the Cuckoo's Nest.

Following a period of work that often divided audiences and critics — notably his turn as the novelist-turned-psychopath in Stanley Kubrick's The Shining, *which bordered on self-parody — he earned a second Oscar for his supporting role as a burned-out astronaut in* Terms of Endearment, *and his career was back on track. More recently he has garnered plaudits for his performances as a moronic hit man in* Prizzi's Honor, *the devil incarnate in* The Witches of Eastwick *and the baseball player-turned-alcoholic of William Kennedy's Pulitzer Prize-winning* Ironweed — *which won him yet another Oscar nomina-tion.*

Nicholson's highly-charged screen presence and notorious "killer smile" belie his easy-going personality. He has a casual down-to-earth manner and a wry sense of humor that immediately put an interviewer at ease; within minutes, you feel as comfortable chatting with him as you would an old friend.

When I started acting, I wanted to be an original. I didn't really want to copy anyone, although sometimes you do whether you want to or not. People ask why it took so long to get started — I think anyone who's not like someone else has a more difficult time getting started. Most people like imitations. It might have been easier that way, but in the long run it would have been disastrous.

I've never accepted anyone else's limitations. If you're acting in a script that isn't sublime, you're not going to transcend it by that much. My early work was largely economic expediency, and wanting to learn how to do it. No one is instinctively born to it.

I think I've learned a lot about acting by doing it and I've always felt an actor had to work in order to learn. I didn't turn down anything in the beginning, or very little. The creative freedom there would be in how you interpret it. They bought me cheap and I wanted to work, so it was a fair trade.

I played Peter Lorre's son in *The Raven*. He'd done all these pictures with Humphrey Bogart, and I used to try and pump him for Bogart stories. Peter was very good to me; he gave me a lot to work with. Boris Karloff was always very interesting when he talked, and Vincent Price was very kind to my mother, who was an amateur painter. They all helped me out. But Roger Corman told me, whatever the scene was, I couldn't be funnier than they were. That was my key for the picture.

I was pretty funny in *The Terror*, with Karloff. That was about the only early picture I got bad reviews for. The best one was, someone said I was "as wooden as Epping Forest." I haven't responded awfully strongly to bad reviews; I have been delighted by good ones sometimes. To know you specifically communicated something and someone not only received it but received it well enough to articulate it back, is very satisfying.

I've liked most of the performances I've given since *Easy Rider*. Each role presents a different challenge. *The King of Marvin Gardens* was difficult because it was kind of a confined person, what I would call "a one-room individual." David Staebler was an introverted character, and yet he had to express a lot, so I had to find new ways to express big things through a small person and that was a challenge. You always wonder if you're doing enough.

With friend Bruce Dern in Bob Rafelson's *The King of Marvin Gardens* (1973).

With Art Garfunkel in Jules Feiffer's *Carnal Knowledge* (1971).

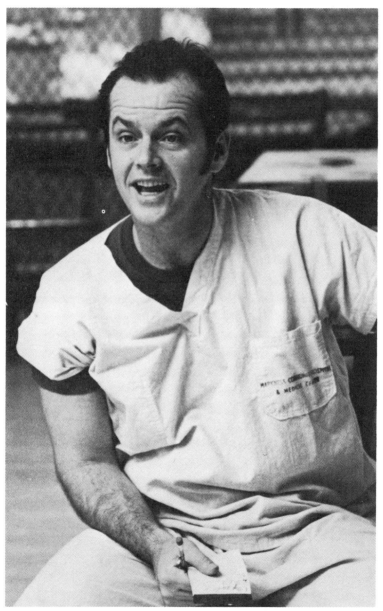

Nicholson earned his first Oscar as the rebellious Randle Patrick McMurphy in *One Flew Over the Cuckoo's Nest* (1975).

David's emotional tract, the end product, is probably less like me than other characters. A lot of his logic is not that foreign to me, but neither am I really close to a concert pianist working in an oil field [*Five Easy Pieces*], or a drunken Southern lawyer [*Easy Rider*]. I haven't played anybody who is really me in films, and I probably won't.

A lot of my ideas about acting have to do with keeping secrets for yourself, things that you don't necessarily act out. I'm not always extremely articulate about what I do, but I try and see what the actual realities of the script are. I try to find orchestrated progressions within scenes, and then make connections and so forth.

I rehearsed the piano work for a couple of months before *Five Easy Pieces*, as much for that as just to get the feeling of someone who had spent a lot of time at the piano. I also checked out the mannerisms of my coach — any little behavior, as much as you can get.

Carnal Knowledge had a kind of skeletal quality to it. It was written by Jules Feiffer and it had his kind of reality from the very beginning; there was a certain fleshing out that needed to be done. Mike Nichols' influence on me was very strong and helped shape that character. It wasn't necessarily a performance I would have given on my own.

On *Chinatown* I had a specific problem in that I feel a detective really has to stay very clean and not seem to be up to what he's up to, but very observant. During that period I just kind of got into a habit of checking out what everyone was wearing, where they were in the room — I wasn't on any cases, so I had to practice that kind of behavior without really showing it—and yet, you can't do something that's completely invisible.

Polanski's basic technique in that film is that the camera is moving pretty much constantly with the people. In order to make it look like that's not what's happening, it becomes very precise and complicated so that it doesn't draw attention to itself. The

With Christopher Lloyd, Richard Bradford and John Belushi in *Goin' South*, directed by Nicholson.

With Jessica Lange on the set of *The Postman Always Rings Twice* (1981).

directing of me that Roman would have to do was always primarily something technical or his helping me work out something; we never had much conflict over my job.

Antonioni and I didn't have much exchange between us on *The Passenger*. He sort of views actors as moving space. They're not always the most important thing in the scene. He has a pretty unorthodox approach. He likes the shooting of each scene to be a documentary on the scene itself; he tries not to know anything about it before it's done.

Working with Antonioni requires a lot of discipline, but I liked it. I'm working with the best directors in the world — it's tough to go wrong. Of all of them, Bob Rafelson is the most overtly interested in performances. He has certain ideas and he'll dig at you a little bit.

Acting is an extremely collaborative art form; a lot depends on who you work with. Most of the actors that I've worked with are good actors and they're on target. The only thing in the scene that's unpredictable is the human being. Everything else is predetermined — the shot, the lighting, the sound — so the only place for something to happen right now is between the human beings related to the environment.

I try and use whatever is really happening right now. I don't let the script be the dominant factor in a piece of work. If I think a scene is happy and I happen to be angry, I don't immediately try to make myself happy. I make sure that anger is not coming from the subconscious as a better interpretation of the scene. Craft is really being able to relax so that the unpredictable in the subconscious can come forward through you.

When you've been acting for this long, you don't remember what you've learned or what you knew... you have to maintain a certain kind of naïveté to be creative and not pre-conditioned, but at the same time you don't go off on a lot of blind alleys.

Donald Sutherland

Donald Sutherland has had one of the most erratic film careers of any contemporary actor. In the sixties, he did bit parts and voice-overs; in the seventies he zigzagged across continents and time zones, shifting from starring roles in box office hits to enigmatic art films rarely seen by the general public. In the eighties, he has gravitated toward intelligent leading man-type parts in films of uneven quality, in favor of the offbeat characters he once relished. While he has never enjoyed the sort of acclaim Jack Nicholson has received, he has done it all with equal finesse.

Donald McNichol Sutherland was born July 17, 1935, in St. John, New Brunswick, Canada, and grew up in Nova Scotia. At age 10, he aspired to be a sculptor and began making puppets; at 14 he became the youngest radio announcer in Canada. He played Scrooge in a high school production of A Christmas Carol *before enrolling in the University of Toronto to study engineering.*

The young student soon switched his major to English and began to consider an acting career. He followed two seasons of summer stock with two years of training at the London Academy of Music and Dramatic Art, then toured Britain with the Perth Repertory Theatre.

Sutherland made a number of appearances on the London stage, beginning with August for the People *with Rex Harrison. In 1964 he made his film debut in* Castle of the Living Dead, *playing a witch and a policeman; other early European films included* Dr. Terror's House of Horrors. *He also played various roles on British television, including Fortinbras in Christopher Plummer's* Hamlet at Elsinore.

The actor made a strong impression in his first American film, The Dirty Dozen *(1967), as a moronic killer who imitates a general inspecting his troops. Three years later he played the irreverent army surgeon, Hawkeye Pierce, in the film version of* M*A*S*H, *which brought star-*

dom to Sutherland and co-star Elliott Gould and inspired the long-running TV series.

Sutherland then made a series of films in which he played long-haired, bearded, spaced-out characters. Contrary to popular opinion, he was not "stoned" during the making of them: "The only time I tried it was with Paul Mazursky on Alex in Wonderland. He gave me a joint to smoke; it didn't aid my concentration at all." Nevertheless, the actor's penchant for peculiar characters created a screen persona that dogged him for years.

He went through another phase in the seventies during which he made a group of esoteric films for European directors, including Nicolas Roeg (Don't Look Now), who "taught me, finally, that I had to make a decision to put my trust in the director"; John Schlesinger (The Day of the Locust); Bernardo Bertolucci (1900); Claude Chabrol (Blood Relatives); and Federico Fellini, who redesigned his face for Fellini's Casanova ("If anybody else had suggested the part I should probably have told them they were crazy.")

Invasion of the Body Snatchers (1978) marked another turning point in Sutherland's career — a decision to play less bizarre characters in films of broader appeal. He received some of the best notices of his career for his performance as Calvin Jarrett, the head of the emotionally distraught family in Ordinary People; his portrayal of artificial heart transplant pioneer Dr. Vrain, in Threshold, won him a Genie Award (the Canadian Oscar) as Best Actor in 1983.

While Sutherland's return to the stage in Lolita was a flop, he continues to work seemingly non-stop in films; in recent months he has been seen as Gauguin in The Wolf at the Door, a priest in The Rosary Murders and a faith healer in Apprentice to Murder. Meanwhile, his young son Kiefer, who bears a striking resemblance to his father, is beginning to emerge as a film star in his own right.

Sutherland seems to enjoy interviews but "I don't like to read them because I'm generally not as precise and witty as I'd like to be." He manages to ask nearly as many questions about his interviewer as one

As Reverend Dupas, with *M*A*S*H* co-star Elliott Gould in Jules Feiffer's *Little Murders* (1971).

As Calvin Jarrett, with Mary Tyler Moore in *Ordinary People*.

asks about him, out of genuine curiosity. He was interviewed prior to the start of production on Ordinary People *in the Los Angeles office of his company, McNichol Pictures.*

When I was 16, I asked my mother if I was good looking. I remember watching her face go absolutely white when she knew she had to confront something that she didn't want to; I wished I'd never asked the question. She said, "No. But your face has a lot of character."

When I was doing television in England, and little bits in movies, they would always hire me to play the homocidal artist; they wouldn't hire me for anything else. There was a film I wanted to do called *Three in the Morning*, and I thought I was perfect for the role. They turned me down on the basis that they wanted someone who looked like the guy next door, and that I didn't look like I ever lived next door to anybody.

I enjoy playing a straight part, like the guy in *M*A*S*H*. Someone who has some kind of sense of humor. But after *M*A*S*H* and *Klute*, with the exception of *Don't Look Now* everything that I played was — I don't know if they were stoned, but the characters were certainly off-the-wall.

I don't see myself as Cary Grant or Clark Gable, but I see myself as playing roles where you can say, "That's a perfect role for him" — not as a character actor, but as an actor performing a character which is close to one's self. The character most like me is in *Invasion of the Body Snatchers*. He was the closest to the guy who lives in my house. The character in *Don't Look Now* was also a lot like me.

I have found gradually over the years that there is more truth in getting as close to the center of myself as I can, as opposed to a character — even though he has a center, a lot of the exterior is applied from observation. I would rather that the observations

26

were fed into the interior, and recreated that way, simply through myself.

When Bob Aldrich asked me to impersonate a general in *The Dirty Dozen*, it wasn't the part I was supposed to play. Clint Walker was supposed to do it; his character was an Indian and he thought it was disparaging to the Indian people. Aldrich looked at me and said, "You with the big ears — you do it." I knew then, it was a shot. I was 30 years old, and it was a chance to get yourself in a position where you'd be able to work.

I feel I've been very lucky. It's very difficult for anyone to be given the freedom and latitude that I've been given, to do just exactly whatever I wanted. I don't think anyone's been allowed as many failures as I have. There were a lot of artistic successes between *Klute* and *Body Snatchers*, but they were certainly all commercial failures.

It didn't concern me, actually; it didn't really make any difference. I was working all the time. There were people telling me, "You shouldn't be doing this; you should be doing this, this and that." And I said, "I don't want to." I've been able to do exactly as I wanted, against everyone's good advice.

It's really the reverse of most people's careers. Most people start out straight and develop; I started from the other end. I feel more like a Giacometti sculpture. You know his sculptures, where he tore them down? He started with fat people, and they ended up being thin as sticks but full of extraordinary energy. That's basically what I'm trying to do.

All the people I've played were based in emotion, really gut raw emotion. Now I would like to base them in a kind of intelligence, so that behind their eyes is a wit and a slyness... there's not a huge difference, but for me as a performer there's a difference. The pace is different. The center is different, more in the brain than in the diaphragm.

It would have been nice to come to the decision I've come to

Still "a little bit off the wall" as Agar, a Victorian pickpocket, in *The Great Train Robbery* (1979).

now, just after *M*A*S*H*. But my work is better and more precise now, and I don't have anything to work off. I don't have anything to get rid of any more — I've done it. But I'd work with Fellini again. *Casanova* was a highpoint for me.

Acting is very subjective work; you depend on everyone else. As a cinema actor, all you're doing is providing the director with the putty that he can use to make his film. On *Day of the Locust* I told John Schlesinger there was something I didn't understand. He said, "Don't worry about it; it's not your job. I'll fix it in the cutting room." But I don't believe that. I think if an actor understands completely what a director wants, he can contribute a lot.

M*A*S*H and *Klute* were films where the director had a specific idea, which I didn't particularly understand, nor was I particularly interested in. All I was interested in was what I thought my character was. I fought with Alan Pakula a lot; there were things in *Klute* which didn't make any sense in terms of movies. I was very naïve and young for my rather elderly years.

I would like very carefully to know the director now, and to know what he wants. Phil Kaufman [*Body Snatchers*] you just sit down with five minutes and you know. Michael Crichton [*The Great Train Robbery*] was so tall I never really did get to know him. Fellini you know you can't trust, so that's the same thing as trusting him.

If you're working with Fellini, you just do as he says. If it's somebody else — I prefer it to be a good relationship; I don't want to step on their toes but I don't want anyone stepping on mine. Up front, we should understand what we want from the picture. What I want is very specific in terms of the way I want to present myself, so that has to be satisfied. If that's the director's intent as well, terrific.

Jack Lemmon

Few actors have been as fortunate as Jack Lemmon — as far as he's concerned — in the choice of roles they have been offered during the course of their career. A two-time Academy Award winner, he is one of the most consistent actors around in the quality of his work; yet, his success has not gone to his head. Asked how he has grown as an artist, he quickly retorts, "Shorter. Shrunk a little."

It is a telling remark, a keen example of the self-effacing wit and down-to-earth manner that is characteristic of Lemmon off-screen. He has no delusions of grandeur, despite the heights he has scaled in his profession. When asked how he approaches his work, in an interview at his Beverly Hills office, he responded, "We'll get deep-dish now and bore the shit out of everybody, but I don't know how else to discuss it. That's an awful danger, actors taking themselves seriously..."

John Uhler Lemmon III was born in Boston on February 8, 1925. At the age of 4, he appeared with his father in an amateur production of Gold in Them Thar Hills, *and the die was cast; at 21 he graduated from Harvard and "promptly headed for New York to save the American theatre." Instead he wound up in a new medium called television, appearing in over 300 live shows; among the earliest was "the first sitcom ever" (*That Wonderful Guy*), in which he co-starred with his future wife, Cynthia Stone.*

In 1953 Lemmon made his Broadway debut in a less-than-memorable revival of Room Service *and his film debut opposite Judy Holliday in* It Should Happen to You. *Two years and four pictures later, his portrayal of the mischievous Ensign Pulver in the film version of* Mister Roberts *won him the Academy Award for Best Supporting Actor.*

Among his favorite screen roles are Jerry/Daphne, the fiddle player in the all-girl band in Some Like It Hot *and C.C. Baxter, the naive young office schnook of* The Apartment *(two of the seven films he has made for writer-director Billy Wilder); the troubled alcoholic of* Days of Wine and Roses; *Felix Ungar, the prissy gourmet of* The Odd Couple; *Harry Stoner, the disillusioned businessman of* Save the Tiger — *for which he won the Oscar as Best Actor; the dissident engineer in* The China Syndrome; *and Ed Horman, the father in search of his son in Costa-Gavras' true-life drama,* Missing.

Unlike most one-time stage actors who achieve success in films, Lemmon has not forsaken the theatre. Undaunted by his second Broadway flop, Face of a Hero *(which one critic dubbed "Trace of a Zero"), he returned to the stage in* Idiot's Delight *and* Juno and the Paycock *(both in Los Angeles),* Tribute *(which he reprised on film) and, most recently, played James Tyrone in* Long Day's Journey Into Night *(in New York and London).*

The actor won an Emmy for S'Wonderful, S'Marvelous, S'Gershwin *and an nomination for his portrayal of Archie Rice in NBC's* The Entertainer *(which he undertook at the suggestion of Laurence Olivier, who created the role). Lemmon has narrated a series of television specials on environmental pollution, including* Plutonium: Element of Risk *for public TV. He has also appeared in a number of documentaries, including a tribute to Ernie Kovacs and a French salute to Billy Wilder entitled* Portrait of a 60% Perfect Man.

Lemmon himself has been honored several times in recent years. In 1986 the bipartisan Congressional Arts Caucus paid tribute to him for his body of work. "Jack Lemmon has held a mirror up in front of us and shown us what we look like with love and affection," said caucus chairman Rep. Tom Downey. "He has shown us that nobody's triumph is minor, and nobody's defeat is insignificant."

More recently, Lemmon received the prestigious Life Achievement Award from the American Film Institute. The actor, who celebrated 25 years of marriage in 1987 to his second wife, actress Felicia Farr, has two children; son Chris, who has followed in his father's footsteps, and daughter Courtney.

As C.C. Baxter, with the much-in-demand key to *The Apartment*.

An image comes [on screen] not only because the public finds it, or assumes it, but because you're pushed into it. If you don't, yourself, fight to bust it, you'll be in a mold. When I first came to Hollywood, I had a seven- year contract. I had to do two pictures a year for Columbia, though it wasn't an exclusive contract. The first couple I did were comedies and then — bang! *Mister Roberts* — that was a big smash. Then 90% of the scripts the studios offered me were comedies.

It took over a year to sell *Days of Wine and Roses* because they thought I was crazy. The studios would let me do anything I wanted, but not a downbeat drama. They thought it was the every-actor-wants-to-play-Hamlet syndrome, which was not true; I was just an actor, I'd played both. I'm damned lucky *Wine and Roses* happened by then, and then *Save the Tiger* helped a lot. I'm very fortunate not to have been labeled a comedic actor.

I've found that the performances that have turned out — at least in other people's opinions — the best for me, almost invariably I have been very afraid to do. Which is enough to make me do it, because I don't want to live with the fact that I copped out.

I was afraid of *Wine and Roses*, I was afraid of *Save the Tiger*, in a sense I was afraid of *Some Like It Hot* because nobody in Hollywood felt that picture had a prayer. They all thought Billy Wilder was crazy, that he had a five-minute burlesque sketch he was going to try to blow up into a two-hour farce, with his two leading men running around in drag. They thought he was insane. The damn thing's a classic. Billy was at the top of his form — he never made a wrong move.

Billy knows precisely what he wants before any camera ever turns. The script is the bible, and God help ya if you start to fool around with the words. And I mean an "and," an "if" or a "but." You do not change a damn thing. *Some Like It Hot* was the only time in seven films that I've ever fucked around with a word. But you don't have to. It's like ad-libbing Shakespeare; it doesn't turn out the same.

Obviously, there's a great respect of the man's authority and the feeling that the sonuvabitch knows what he's talking about. Billy can also be a fooler, and about halfway through *Some Like It Hot* I learned a great lesson about listening to a director. When I come into the room and tell Tony Curtis "I'm engaged" — to Joe E. Brown — I had worked that mother out, I couldn't wait. I knew it was a great scene.

I came on the set and Billy Wilder hands me these maracas and says, "In between the lines, because you're so excited, you do a dance and you shake the maracas." I got sick to my stomach; I said, "The man is crazy." But he'd come up with a genius thing: if I had not done that and broken it up between each line, you wouldn't have heard a damn thing from then on.

I think that film, in many ways, for an audience is the greatest of mediums 'cause it's limitless; there's nothing you can't do. I'm constantly stunned, working in film and seeing a film as it progresses... at what can be done, the magic that can be created.

There's a quality of believability. And the audience very often, more often I think than in the theatre, gets totally involved. It's a quality like the old days of live television at its best, of immediacy. It's hardly immediate but if you can make it seem that it's happening for the first time you can get that quality.

Live TV was kind of half way between film and stage. That was heaven in a sense because it combines both of these things. You didn't have the audience but it was sustained, and there were cameras. I think if you're basically a stage actor as I was, and you have the desire... it's *good* to go back and stretch yourself and to give a sustained performance, instead of falling into the use of technique — which is easy to do without realizing it in front of a camera. It goes back to that syndrome of a Jack Lemmon image.

If I read one more article about an actor who has been primarily involved in films, who then decides to do a play, and starts talking about the greatness of theatre as opposed to film, I'm

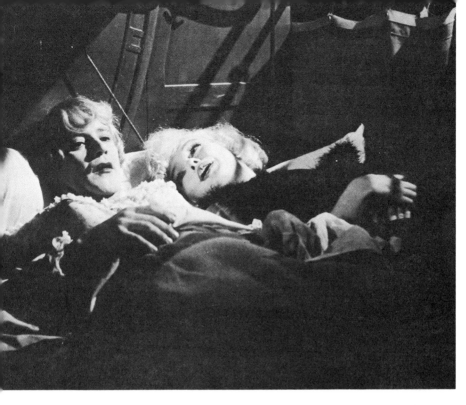

Lemmon in drag, with Marilyn Monroe turning up the heat, in Billy Wilder's *Some Like It Hot* (1959); with Matthau and Wilder on the set of *The Front Page* (1974).

As Felix, with Walter Matthau as Oscar, in Neil Simon's *The Odd Couple* (1968); with Sandy Dennis and a newly-chipped tooth, in Simon's *The Out-of-Towners* (1970).

gonna vomit. I love film, and I love the stage and they are radically different in their appeals.

Peculiarly enough I think it is in general more difficult to give a comparably good performance in film, than on stage — by a long shot. First of all, you do not have the audience to tell you — and boy, can they tell you. You have no audience and you're shooting out of sequence. Several key and highly emotional scenes in *Wine and Roses* were chopped up into bits and pieces; at times I would have to pick up a scene in the middle on a very high hysterical note without having the opportunity to start the scene from the beginning and logically build to that peak.

You have to do a helluva lot more homework in film 'cause you don't know what in the hell you're going to shoot. *Save the Tiger* is the only film I know of that was shot in sequence. The entire cast stayed until we got to their scenes; we rehearsed on the locations and we shot in sequence. That was such a luxury. But in film you can't do it.

The trick I learned, whatever scene I'm doing, I'm not working on that anywhere near as much as the scene prior to that, and maybe two scenes prior, to make damn sure I know where I'm going and in my mind trying to see the progress, the growth of a character. On the stage you start with the curtain going up and you keep going.

I was nine years old when I first dreamed of having a Broadway hit — I was 53 when it happened. I wasn't looking for a play when *Tribute* arrived. It was the right timing. It had what I look for and so seldom find — you cannot label it, which we tend to want to do with everything. You can't label life either.

In *Tribute* we have a fella who never really pinpointed his talents, who's got it all but never really applied himself. So why should we be concerned? This is the fascination of the play: why should we care so much for this not-extraordinary man? Except hopefully by the end, he is. If we don't care about him, then why should we give a shit about anybody, unless they're Einstein? The role was a challenge; I didn't know how to play it. If I did there wouldn't have been anything to it.

There is a lot to be said about instinct. As you get older and more in control of your craft and technique, and you have lived longer, you don't have to do certain things; they happen. They wouldn't happen if you didn't know what you were doing.

I have pleased myself sometimes, very often not completely but certainly at moments, in a performance where I feel there is a maturity, and there is the ability to be simpler, to do less, not to be by any means "Jack Lemmon" — whatever that image is — especially in *The China Syndrome*.

I loved working with Jim Bridges on *China Syndrome*. We would do a scene and he would say, "That's a print, that's perfect. Let's do one more." And then he would say, "Navy." That's all he would say. But the image to me of a naval officer, which this character once was — by the book — contains you and pulls you in. You don't show as much; it stays inside. That was the key piece of direction that he gave me all through the picture. It's like saying "less," which usually is better. Everything good is simple. It's trying to be simple that's so involved.

Peter Sellers

Peter Sellers was never shadowed by a pre-conceived image, as Jack Lemmon has been through much of his career; he was a cinematic chameleon who altered not only his personality but his entire physiognomy from one role to another.

When Sellers joked on television, "there is no me... there used to be a me, but I had it surgically removed" — he may have been telling the truth. He seemed to lose himself in the characters he played, particularly the accident-prone Inspector Clouseau of the popular Pink Panther *series, which began in 1964. (Ironically, the role was intended for Peter Ustinov.)*

Peter Richard Henry Sellers was born September 8, 1925, in Southsea, England, the son of vaudeville performers. He made his public debut two weeks later, when he was carried onto the stage of the King's Theatre in Portsmouth; he promptly burst into tears, and the audience laughed. In his teens he aspired to become a drummer, and played one-night stands with a succession of bands.

During World War II, Sellers served as an armorer in India and the Middle East, entertaining at camp concerts during off hours. After the war, the struggling comic toured in vaudeville and did a stint in a strip-tease emporium, which instilled new confidence in him. He then brashly phoned a BBC Radio producer and impersonated two well known comedians, recommending "a marvelous young comic" named Sellers. A five-minute guest spot on a variety program called Show Time *soon led to a flurry of bookings.*

In 1951 he teamed with Spike Milligan and Harry Secombe on The Goon Show, *which introduced British audiences to a new high — or low — in irreverent humor. Sellers, who made his film debut the same year, was often heard but seldom seen in those days; he impersonated*

Humphrey Bogart for some additional dialogue on Beat the Devil *and did the off-screen voice of Churchill in* The Man Who Never Was. *Film audiences first took notice when he appeared in* The Ladykillers *with Alec Guinness, who befriended him and regarded him as a protégé.*

Sellers bounced from one characterization to another with uncanny precision and dazzling speed in the late fifties and early sixties, among them a shop steward in I'm All Right, Jack; *the prim and proper Grand Duchess (one of three roles) in* The Mouse That Roared; *and the protean Quilty of Stanley Kubrick's* Lolita. *Sellers' tour de force as mild-mannered U.S. President Muffley, insecure RAF captain Mandrake and the crazed nuclear scientist of the title in Kubrick's* Dr. Strangelove *(1964) earned him an Oscar nomination.*

The comic's portrayal of an bumbling Indian actor in Blake Edwards' The Party *— which has become a cult film — was followed by a lengthy succession of uninspired work; even the occasional good performance (*The Optimists of Nine Elms*) went unnoticed. Sellers' and Edwards' careers were finally rescued by the huge box office success of* The Return of the Pink Panther *and two additional sequels.*

While actor and director both had insisted they would have nothing to do with each other, Edwards observed, "It's the old Hollywood bullshit thing. I'll never work with that son of a bitch again ...until I need him."

The comedian spent nearly a decade trying to convince Jerzy Kosinski to sell the film rights to Being There *before the Polish novelist relented. The comic fable, directed by Hal Ashby, starred Sellers as Chance, an illiterate, simple-minded gardener who becomes the toast of Washington high society. It was the culmination of his career.*

Sellers kept largely to himself on the set during filming, and remained in character between scenes. During the last week of production, he remarked — perhaps only half in jest — that in the event he won the Oscar for Best Actor, "I plan to send a hunchbacked dwarf to collect the award." He lost to Dustin Hoffman.

As the inept Tully Bascombe in *The Mouse That Roared* (1959), above; and the spectacularly uncoordinated Inspector Clouseau in *A Shot in the Dark* (1964).

As President Muffley, with Stanley Kubrick on the set of *Dr. Stranglove* (1964).

With director Hal Ashby during the filming of *Being There* (1979).

I started out with a run of successes. I had eight smash hits in a row; every film I did, couldn't go wrong. Then every film I did went wrong. I always thought it was going to do that; it couldn't go on forever. I wondered how many flops I could sustain. I had six or seven years of one flop after another before *The Return of the Pink Panther*. I was getting to the stage where people were crossing the road so they wouldn't have to embarrass themselves by saying hello.

This business breeds a certain kind of people. If you're making films, and the films are making money — I literally think they would eat your shit. I absolutely detest these people.

I had no idea these *Pink Panther* things were going to take off in such a way. I'm continually amazed at these things. I always try to make product that feels right to me, although I must say… the *Panther* films are made for an audience. If you put one on and you didn't do what they wanted you to do, they'd come out bitterly disappointed.

When I was in radio years ago and we did *The Goon Show* — very far out and sort of intellectual humor — we used to appeal to a very small minority group, a hardcore minority that grew. But the *Panther* films appeal to a mass audience; the grown-ups laugh at them as much as the kids do.

People enjoy having an absolutely hysterical laugh. I do myself. I like to scour the papers for a good comedy; I want to see something that will really tickle me and amuse me. I think the people who spend the night out at the cinema, they want to laugh. They're much hungrier these days then they were when we made the original *Pink Panther*. They were saturated with Doris Day films then.

I believe shooting had already started on the first film before I was cast. I discussed the character of Inspector Clouseau with Blake Edwards, outlining the form he would take. As he existed on paper, he would have been played by Peter Ustinov entirely differently.

I was out to create something away from the traditional idea of the Hercule Poirot-type of French or Belgian detective; after discussion with Blake, we hit on something we thought we'd experiment with, and it seemed to be right. So we continued along those lines.

I don't think we were aware of injecting any physical comedy into it at the time, but as Clouseau came to life and began to take on his own personality it developed that he was rather accident-prone, hiding it under a great cloak of dignity and seriousness — as most people who are that way usually do. They tend to fly a kite in another direction so that your attention will be diverted.

I think people enjoy somebody making a twit of themselves. From school on, for the rest of your life it seems they're waiting around the corner for you to fall over, or do something stupid. Then of course there's hero worship, where they try to protect you — but there never has been in my case. They were always waiting around the corner for me to do something.

I don't know why it's funny. It's very difficult to dissect comedy. If you ask me why Laurel and Hardy are funny, I can only say, they appeal to me as people; their presence makes me laugh. Blake Edwards and I are both very keen fans of Laurel and Hardy, and we quite unashamedly take some of their routines and fit them to our films; there's a lot of Laurel and Hardy in the Clouseau films.

Clouseau I've based, to some extent, in manner of speech anyway, on this concierge I once came across in a hotel in Paris. If a guest wanted something to be done, he'd wait for the guest to say what it was he wanted. Then he just repeated what the guy had asked him to do. And he gave the concierge $100 for doing nothing, just repeating it. I watched this fellow and that was his modus operandi.

I do that a lot with Clouseau. For instance with the phrase, "Yes, I know that." Clouseau always wants to be right in the

An unscripted moment in *Dr. Strangelove* that "just happened."

Sellers as Inspector Clouseau, disguised as Toulouse-Lautrec, in *The Revenge of the Pink Panther* (1978).

picture. In *A Shot in the Dark*, the butler said in one scene, "Telephone call for you, Inspector Clouseau." He said, "Ah, yes, that will be for me."

There's a lot of improv. Not so much as in a Stanley Kubrick movie, where you're encouraged to improvise a great deal, but if Blake and I feel something doesn't work for Clouseau then we have to find a way around it — and that's the way we usually work.

Blake and I both find that working conditions are difficult when we're trying to think up something or create something. I never have any problem with other directors and he doesn't have any problem with other actors. I never had any problem with Kubrick. I made two movies with him; we got on like a house on fire. Just absolutely eye to eye.

That thing just happened in *Dr. Strangelove*, where I'm strangling myself. It wasn't planned or anything. I remember Stanley saying, "Jesus, we must get two cameras on that. Do that with your hand again." I recognized the film as a great work of art by Stanley but I hated what I'd done myself.

I've never been able to look at my own work objectively, I'm afraid. I find it very difficult to watch myself. I have to be careful; I could come out with such depression I'd leave the business. I get so down about it. The satisfaction is in the moment you do the work, not before it, not after it.

I never can approach the perfection I'm aiming at. I am a perfectionist and I can never reach it; it thwarts me and enrages me and I get so upset, I have no idea how one can continue... all I know is, I'm filled with this ghastly horror, partly because when I've seen myself on the screen it was so awful. I suppose if I looked like Errol Flynn it would help a lot. I sometimes wonder how other people manage, but they do.

Peter Sellers died July 24, 1980 in a London hospital, following a massive heart attack. He was 54 years old.

Reginald Owen

Stage and screen performer Reginald Owen was much a nineteenth-century man who felt he had lived beyond his time. "There's no romance left in the theatre," he lamented in an interview at his Beverly Hills home, two years before his death. "The world's gone too quick, too fast. Nobody cares about anything. The lovely things about a woman are forgotten now; it's only whether they can be shown nude or not. Everything else has gone by..."

In a career that spanned seven decades, the venerable character actor played a wide variety of roles, but never realized an ambition to play Hamlet. "I don't think I would have been a particularly good Hamlet, but I wouldn't have been too bad a Hamlet," he observed. The actor, who was virtually weaned on Dickens as a child, regarded Scrooge in A Christmas Carol *as his favorite role; the 1938 MGM film has been a holiday perennial for half a century, despite a number of remakes.*

John Reginald Owen was born in Wheathampstead, Hertfordshire, England, on August 5, 1887. While attending Tree's Academy of Acting (now the Royal Academy of Dramatic Art) he began performing at the famed Her Majesty's Theatre (now His Majesty's) in London's West End; in 1905 the first-year pupil won a gold medal for his performance in The Tempest.

Twenty years and fifty-odd roles later, he made his New York stage debut in The Carolinian, *and the following year starred as Algernon in* The Importance of Being Earnest. *He was playing Cardinal Richelieu in Ziegfeld's production of* The Three Musketeers *when he was asked to make a screen test, which resulted in his first American film; he followed the three-reel* Pusher-in-the-Face *immediately with* The Letter, *and went on to become one of Hollywood's top supporting players.*

The only actor ever to play both Sherlock Holmes and Dr. Watson on film, Owen portrayed the popular detective in the low-budget A Study in Scarlet — for which he helped write the script — and the sleuth's venerable colleague in the 1932 Sherlock Holmes, which was set in modern day London.

During a 16-year stint in the Metro-Goldwyn-Mayer stock company he appeared in such classics as Anna Karenina, A Tale of Two Cities, Woman of the Year, Mrs. Miniver, Random Harvest and National Velvet. Among his later efforts were the Moral Rearmament film, Voice of the Hurricane, and Disney's Mary Poppins, as Admiral Boom.

Owen wrote two plays and several books, but did not live, as he had hoped, to make a recording of historic speeches including the Sermon on the Mount. "It's a tough assignment for any actor to be asked to play Jesus Christ," he noted, "but you hope that the spirit of Christ will come to you and there will be a moment that you may be able to deliver it as it should be delivered."

His final projects were somewhat less sublime: Disney's Bedknobs and Broomsticks, and a stage revival of A Funny Thing Happened On the Way to the Forum that starred Phil Silvers.

At school in London we had to give recitations and things. We had a prize day every year that was presided over by the Lord Mayor of London. We did scenes from Shakespeare and different things and I used to get prizes for that. I was a very good elocutionist in those days.

I was 16 when I read in *The Times* an advertisement saying that Sir Herbert Beerbohm Tree was forming a school of dramatic art. So I learned a long poem and I went to Her Majesty's Theatre. Tree was there and an old actress named Mrs. Bakeman Crow and one of the leading men of the time, he was called Handsome Jack Barnes; he wasn't too handsome because he had become older and he was rather fat. And I did my recitation. I spoke

As Dr. Watson, with Clive Brook in *Sherlock Holmes* (1932).

With Margaret Sullavan in *The Good Fairy*, scripted by Preston Sturges.

two lines and they stopped me; I went back to my parents and told them I had failed because they wouldn't let me say anything.

However, they stopped me because I was so good; three weeks later I joined the class and I was immediately put under contract by Tree. I played small parts at Her Majesty's Theatre and at the same time I did my studies at Tree's Academy. At the end of the year they did this final public hearing of the students — and to my immense surprise, I won the Bancroft Medal, the first gold medal ever given.

When I first started at Her Majesty's, I played the small part of Tom Chitling, one of the thieves in *Oliver Twist*. Tree played Fagin. I had to fall off the back of a chair, or at least I got kicked and I fell over the chair. Tree cooked sausages with a toasting fork and he would come down on me with the fork and hit me on the back.

There were marks on my back and I didn't like it. So in the prop room I found an old tin plate which was used by one of the soldiers in *Julius Caesar*, and I put that under the shirt. That night the time came when I had to expect this blow on the back and I was really looking forward to it — but the result was that Tree bent his toasting fork. And he looked at me — he had an immense sense of humor, Sir Herbert Beerbohm Tree, and I had a bit of a sense of humor too — and we both called it quits.

You've no idea what the theatre was in those days. My mother used to come up from the country to meet me on Wednesdays and we would go to the matinee. I think it was from my mother I got the love of the theatre. I can remember those afternoons when we would go to the matinees; I saw Henry Irving play three or four of his greatest characters. To watch Tree play Svengali was an unforgettable experience.

There were only two mediums of entertainment in those days; the first was the theatre and the second was the stories which came out in magazines like the *Strand Magazine*. My family subscribed always to the *Strand*, and the stories which appeared each month were looked forward to so eagerly. When Conan Doyle wrote the Sherlock Holmes stories, he wrote them at a time when there was no television. There was not even radio, there was only the theatre.

Some years later I'd been to Hollywood and then I'd gone back to New York... and I had to stop at Tiffany-Stahl Studios, where my friend Bob Florey was making a picture. Anyway, Sam Bischoff, the head of Tiffany-Stahl, had bought the Sherlock Holmes story, *A Study in Scarlet*. He couldn't produce it because it had a Mormon theme and that was taboo. So he said to Florey and myself, if you'd like to make a story out of it... Bob would direct and I would play Sherlock Holmes.

Bob thought it was a good idea and very casually wrote on a half sheet of paper an outline of a plot. It was a very funny plot. Then I wrote all the dialogue of it, and I put into it all the characters which I had known as a young man in England; altogether it was very amusing. At the last moment Bob couldn't direct it so Eddie Marin did it and a damn good job he made of it. It was produced I think in about 10 days.

I remember reading an account of it in *Variety*, that the first week it played to $22,000, which in those days was a tremendous amount of money. Then for some unaccountable reason no other bookings took place in America. The reason was that Fox Studios was then producing a picture with Clive Brook as Sherlock Holmes and they asked me to play Watson, which I did. I don't think there was much difference in my characterization.

I think my Sherlock Holmes had a lot of humanity about him, and I'm sure it was good from a public point of view because I had a degree of humor. I don't think that dear old Basil Rathbone... he's so devoid of humor that it really is terrifying.

I think Talleyrand was one of the most interesting characters that I've ever played. The picture was called *Conquest*. Greta Garbo was in it and Charles Boyer played Napoleon. Talleyrand

photo by the author

At his Beverly Hills home in 1970.

was a diplomat; he had these inscrutable eyes and you'd never know what he was thinking. Jack Dawn made the most wonderful makeup for me; he made these eyes which had overlapping lids, if I can use that term.

One day I came to the studio and we were still shooting. Clarence Brown was directing. He was mad; he said, "We've put together a sequence and you don't give one single expression. This damn makeup is simply awful; I've got to shoot it all over again." He said, "Come to the projection room and see what an awful mess it is." He ran this whole sequence and I was fascinated; Talleyrand was magnificent. I said, "To me, it's absolutely perfect." So that seemed to mollify Brown a bit. You were fascinated by the face because you never knew what the man was thinking.

The actor had great freedom in those days. Even when I was under contract at Metro, I always had freedom of a role. I played in one or two "B" pictures in all the years I was there. I see a lot of old pictures on TV, and I'm amazed at the pains that were taken in the pictures in those days. Time is money now and if you play in a television show of any kind, God help you if you don't know your line.

I think years ago actors were much more particular than they are today. I know in my case... I'm a tremendous stickler for getting the thing as well as it can be done; I like to get every period and comma in. If you've got a mind which is adroit enough to improvise, they will probably let you get away with it. But if you are a very meticulous person, as I am, it's a very tough racket.

Reginald Owen died November 5, 1972, of a heart attack in Boise, Idaho. He was 85 years old.

Bill McLinn

There is one candidate for President this year who is virtually beyond reproach, a man of unimpeachable character whose background will withstand the keenest scrutiny — except, perhaps, his own. He has a penchant for candor that has raised more than a few eyebrows, and is his own sharpest critic. His name: Mark Twain.

The late humorist, who died in 1910, has been brought back to life in the person of Bill McLinn, who travels the lecture circuit as Twain. McLinn speaks on social issues, using only Twain's words; he has given speeches tailored to college students and corporate executives, as well as church sermons presenting the author's views on disarmament.

William L. McLinn was born in La Canada, California, in 1943 and now resides in Washington, D.C. A former Congressional staff member, he holds a Master's degree in International Relations, with a focus on Soviet relations and the United Nations. He made unique use of his background when he lectured — as Twain — on "war and peace" during the Geneva arms reduction talks.

"It's ironic, it's sad and a little frightening to realize how much of what he said applies today because things haven't changed that much," observes McLinn. "We are just as stupid now as we were 100 years ago."

The soft-spoken McLinn, a one-time anti-war activist, is an ordained minister and also has a law school degree. He considers himself "an actor/scholar. I don't like the word 'impersonator.' 'Embodiment' is closer, but sort of weird." He is not intimidated by the success of actor Hal Holbrook, whose triumphant one-man show (Mark Twain Tonight!) has been touring for over 30 years.

Drawing on Twain's extant writings, lectures and attributable quotes, McLinn has memorized 15 hours of material from which to draw upon. His performances are unscripted. During the second half of his

photo by Fred Watkins, Capital Cities/ABC, Inc.

McLinn on the lecture circuit, as *Mark Twain Himself.*

show, he brings the house lights up and answers questions from the audience, using Twain's words. He appears frequently on national television, and has performed Mark Twain Himself *on tour in England, India, Japan, China and the Soviet Union, where Twain enjoys huge popularity.*

"As a person, Bill is involved with concerns like world hunger. Twain is a vehicle for him to get a message across to people, in a humorous fashion — the words are Twain's, but the philosophy is Bill's," says his former representative, Garrett Lee. "If he could go around as Bill McLinn, and drop the Twain persona, he would do it in a minute."

I began doing Mark Twain in the fall of 1975, as a graduate school special project at the University of California in Berkeley. I did a half-hour program as Twain for a youth group; it did not go well. A professor who had directed me in a play at Berkeley told me to forget it, unless I wanted to put a lot of time in on it.

But I had about two months free, so I decided to work on it. Fredrick Andersen, the editor of The Mark Twain Papers Collection at Berkeley, helped me with the show.

I read all the news clippings about Twain's appearances. There was no television then, so the newspapers were more graphic in their description — how he looked, how he moved and so forth. Plus I used what other people said about him, and how he described himself. I did not look at newsreels until I'd been doing the show for a while.

Twain had a nasal, high-pitched voice. The late Henry Nash Smith, the dean of Twain scholars, said that both Hal Holbrook and I dropped the "g" on the "ing" of words. He said Twain also dropped the "i" — I am beginning to do that; it is not easy to relearn.

I like Holbrook's show. There are others who do Twain; I have seen some I didn't like. There were people impersonating Twain in his day. He thought that was a kind of compliment. He enjoyed it; in fact, he went to see a couple of them. But he was a little upset when some of them skipped out on their hotel bill, and he would have to pay the tab.

In the realm of theatre, Holbrook is a master; outside the theatre, I have a leg up on him. I'm more flexible, able to do different types of presentations. Twain gave after-dinner speeches, commencement addresses, press conferences and fund-raisers; I do all of that, not just the theatrical performance.

The content is different, too. I deal with social issues as well as tell humorous stories. I have a one hour script giving Twain's views on the arms race, 100 years ago. An hour on racial issues, and different topics like that. Corporations will ask me to tailor a speech to their program — I'll do a motivational type speech. I've done Twain for philosophy and political science classes too. I do the "whitewashing the fence" story from *Tom Sawyer*. It's a very philosophical piece; there are no losers in that story.

There's a message in the show, but it's also motivational, and it's also entertainment. I like to combine them all. I particularly like the question-and-answer sessions — it makes the audience feel like it's their own event. When I open for questions, I will break character and talk as myself, as well as Twain.

Mark Twain and I have a lot of common ideas and philosophies. His style of humor and mine are similar, except that mine is not as polished perhaps. But we both prefer the dry, British-type humor.

A young, conservative Republican once asked me to speak about the President at a dinner in St. Louis. I said he was a "cheap imitation cowboy," and I continued in that vein, using Twain's words. Everyone thought I was talking about Reagan, of course, and they began to get a little irritated. Finally I said, "I never did like Teddy Roosevelt" — and the whole place just fell apart.

THAT OLD GANG OF MINE

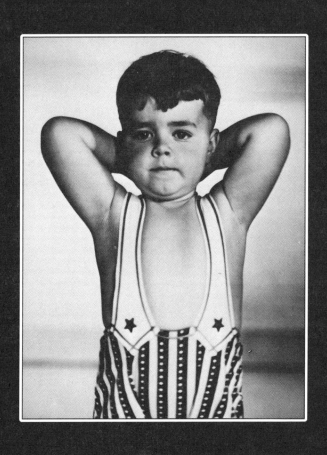

Spanky McFarland

George McFarland is a man who takes pride in his accomplishments, past and present. As Spanky, he was the star of the classic Our Gang Comedies during the 1930s and early '40s. As George, he has had a second and highly successful career as a salesman.

Spanky reminisced at length a few years ago when he visited Los Angeles for a reunion of that old gang of his. "There have been others, but this is the first one I've attended. You have to be an idiot not to like having your ego massaged, and I got it massaged," he observed the next day, in a thick Texas drawl. "Yeah, the lump came in the throat. It was wonderful."

George Robert Phillips McFarland was born October 2, 1928, in Dallas. He appeared in 95 films in the popular Hal Roach series, beginning with Free Eats *— and a five-year contract that called for $75 to $100 a week — in 1932, and concluding with* Unexpected Riches *a decade later. In between he also appeared in a number of features, including the early Technicolor film,* Trail of the Lonesome Pine.

Spanky's popularity and his fame as a child star were exceeded only by Shirley Temple, herself an Our Gang reject. "I wouldn't take a million dollars for the experience," he once said, "and I wouldn't take a penny to do it again."

In the early '50s, the Our Gang series was syndicated to television as The Little Rascals; today, home video has introduced Spanky and his cohorts to yet another new generation of fans — including his granddaughter.

McFarland, who made a cameo appearance as the Governor of Texas in The Aurora Encounter *(1984), lives in Ft. Worth with his wife, Doris. He now travels the college circuit with an evening of films and remembrances and often participates in celebrity golf tournaments.*

I started in Our Gang Comedies at 3. I was the first child in the family and times were tough back then. It was a chance to come to Hollywood and get paid whether you worked or not. There was the glamour, and all that jazz — I'm sure it was attractive to my folks. I was a salable piece of property, and as long as I didn't get hurt, it was a pretty good deal. So we had a go at it. But they weren't stage parents; they didn't push me or anything like that. It just happened.

I started by doing some local advertising in Dallas. I was modeling baby clothes for a department store there, and doing some advertising for a little soft drink company called Dr. Pepper. My aunt sent my picture in to Hal Roach, and he sent for me to make a screen test. I signed a contract and stayed 11 years.

The screen test was used in the comedy called *Spanky*. I was in bed with Pete the Pup, reading a book or something; there was a fly flying around. The fly lit on Pete's head and I bopped him with a rubber hammer. Then they had one of the propmen behind the wall of this bedroom where I was supposed to be, and he had this rubber bug on a wire.

Bob McGowan, my director, says, "Get the hammer, Spanky, and go get the bug." So I get up — I've already wiped out Pete with a shot between the eyes — and every time I would try to hit the bug, the propman would move it. Bob McGowan kept saying, "Hit the bug, Spanky!" And finally I looked up at him and said, "If Don [the propman] will hold the damn thing still, I will!"

There are several stories about the nickname. There was a reporter on the set — as one story goes — he was talking to Mr. McGowan, and he suggested the name. Whether it was because "he looked so spankable" or what, I don't know. My nickname before I came to Hollywood was Sonny.

I grew up in the movies. I thought everybody was in the movies, because that was my world; it was part of my daily life. I didn't know it was unusual for a child to do what I was doing. I only went to school three hours a day. The kids in the neighbor-

Darla Hood, Scotty Beckett, Pete the Pup, Spanky, Baby Sandy,
Buckwheat Thomas and Alfalfa Switzer at Hal Roach Studios, 1935.

Spanky with Laurel and Hardy on the set of *Tit for Tat*.

With comedian Robert Woolsey, of Wheeler and Woolsey, in RKO's
Kentucky Kernels (1935).

hood had to go all day long; I thought I had a license to steal.

And then, as I got older, I realized, "Hey, there's other people out there, and they're not in the movies — I never see them." Then I became aware of what I was doing, and who I was. The blush was off the rose. I would rather have been out fishing or playing ball, but I knew I had to do it. The contract said I had to do it.

The money was good, but it's nothing like today. We spent the hell out of it. There really wasn't that much of it. I guess there was enough to have made some small investments and I might have had a small income from it, but it would've been very small.

When my contract expired with Metro-Goldwyn-Mayer, I was tickled to death. I told my dad and mom, "I don't want to make any more movies." The logical thing would be that Spanky McFarland, large-type star of Our Gang Comedies, should stay in Hollywood and do picture work. Who's to say whether I should have stayed or not? The fact remains that I didn't and we moved back to Texas, and had some very rough times.

I wasn't that impressed with the movies. Chopping wood for the stove to heat the house — I thought that was neat. That was something I'd never done before. As I grew older, the real world became apparent to me. I don't think I ever ignored it; I knew it was there. But I also realized I didn't know how to do anything. All I knew how to do was act. And it was very difficult.

Everybody knew me, Spanky McFarland. I'd go for a job, and instead of talking about the job, they had to talk about Spanky. And half the time — I don't know whether they thought it was beneath my dignity or what — I wouldn't get the job.

I went in the service and did a little stretch there. I came out and it was the old Hollywood story — except it wasn't in Hollywood, it was in Dallas. I sold insurance, I fried hamburgers, I sold Coca Cola, I drove route trucks. I moved back out to Los Angeles. I made popsicles for Arden farms, I pumped gas. Then I moved to Tulsa and had a kid show there; we showed The Little Rascals on the CBS TV affiliate.

At an Our Gang reunion in Los Angeles, 1980.

Probably the turning point was when I went to work for Italian Swiss Colony Wine — that's when I found out I could sell. I was tickled to death with it, and I paid attention to what I was doing and sharpened my abilities. Then I worked for Philco Ford for 10 years, and from there I went to Magic Chef in Fort Worth.

When I realized that I was going have to do something else to make a living and feed the face, I swore that I would never use Spanky to get a job or further whatever career I was going into. Italian Swiss Colony hired George McFarland; they didn't hire Spanky. They didn't know I was Spanky, until later. The same with Philco. Magic Chef knew who I was, but I told them, "I want you to understand, you are hiring George. You are not hiring Spanky. Spanky's not for sale right now."

I don't have any trouble with separation of church and state, so to speak. I keep 'em separate. I use Spanky when it benefits me. I have control over it, and I do it my way. And I'm very proud of that. I've got a George career and a Spanky career; I have a great deal of satisfaction both ways.

I guess the most important thing in my life — I'm not diminishing my career with Our Gang — is the fact that I got out of the movies and ultimately found another way to make a living. I'm dependent upon nobody, and I like that. George did that; Spanky didn't do that.

I would have liked to go to college. But I didn't; I had to go to work. My three children have a college education, and they will do with their lives what they will. I wanted them to have it because I didn't. Not because I think it's that important; it's just something I would like to have had, and I made up my mind that they would never say, "Well, I didn't go to college."

A radio interviewer once asked me why I thought some of the Our Gang kids had such tragic circumstances happen to them. I could blame this and I could blame that; I could spend an hour talking about it. I said, "Well, maybe they stayed at the dance too long." I think that's as good a description as any. I left the dance early and it was a little tough, but I made it — and I think I'm a better man for it.

Huntz Hall

Huntz Hall is one of the survivors of the original Dead End Kids. Like the Our Gang Comedies, the films in which Hall appeared are as popular today as when they were made.

Hall struck it rich playing a kid from the streets, a life not unlike the one he might have led if he hadn't become an actor. "Sach was a true-life character," Hall recalled during an interview in Costa Mesa, California. "There was a kid on my block named Springy; he used to jump. And he walked like I walked. Then there was a man in San Francisco — everything was from life."

Henry Hall was born in New York City on August 15, 1919. As a child actor he got an early taste of fame on radio, appearing on such programs as Bobby Benson's Adventures and Arch Oboler's Rich Kid. He then played Dippy in the landmark Broadway production of Dead End (1935), reprising his role in the film version two years later.

Members of the gang — which included Billy Halop, Leo Gorcey, Gabriel Dell, Bernard Punsley and Bobby Jordan at the outset — came and went as the group evolved, changing monickers and studio affiliations. During a 20-year period, Hall was a member of Warner Bros.' and Universal's Dead End Kids, Universal's Little Tough Guys, Monogram's East Side Kids and Allied Artists' Bowery Boys, of which he eventually became the leader.

Since the popular series ended in 1958, he has immersed himself in the theatre, appearing in such vehicles as Born Yesterday, The Odd Couple and The Sunshine Boys. His films have included Ken Russell's Valentino (in which he played movie pioneer Jesse Lasky), The Escape Artist and more recently, Cyclone.

"If you saw the original script, you'd flip," he says of the offbeat and uneven Valentino. "It was a great piece of work. They cut it all up. That's why I love theatre — they can't do that on stage."

I started when I was three months old. My uncle was a stage-hand; he got me in a play. Before that I was a punk. I didn't like acting when I was a kid. I had an act with five kids in my family, in vaudeville. I was always the objector. My mother would say, "He's never gonna make it." And my father would say, "No, he's the guy. I see it in him. He's a natural."

I was a very religious kid; they thought I was going to be a priest. My son is a priest. When I got out of grammar school, I decided I wanted to go to Professional Children's School. I had gone for a few weeks when Martin Gabel came by one day, at recess.

He said, "Have you tried out for *Dead End*? I said, "Yeah, I lost out." He said, "Come on back." I didn't want to go back. He took me down to where Sidney Kingsley was rehearsing the kids. There was one kid there and he asked him to do the machine gun. The kid said, "Hey look, fellas, I got a machine gun. Di-di-di-di-di." Kingsley had him do the line about 10 times; he got so angry with him, he just looked at me — I was standing in the doorway — and he said, "Can you do a machine gun?" I said, "Yeah." I went, "Rat-tat-tat-tat-tat." He said, "Take the scene."

We were treated like children in Hollywood. If you did anything wrong, the studio bosses would chastise you. They'd come down to the set and talk to you. They were like a father image. They'd give you anything you wanted, but they wouldn't give you money. They wouldn't give you a $50 a week raise, but they'd give you a brand new Buick.

Actors didn't treat us like children. They had respect for us. They loved us and understood us, because we were basically theatre actors. I loved everyone I worked with — Bogart, Cagney, Reagan. I really loved Pat O'Brien. And I adored John Garfield; when he died, part of my heart went. Humphrey Bogart was our idol, after we got to know him. He loved us and we loved him, because he was a kid off the New York streets also.

74

As Dippy (far right) with Sylvia Sydney, James Burke, Billy Halop (foreground), Bernard Punsley and Bobby Jordan in *Dead End (1937)*.

As Sach (left) with Bennie Bartlett, Leo Gorcey, David Gorcey and Bernard Gorcey in *Private Eyes (1953)*.

Michael Curtiz was a genius. He made us sign an agreement when he directed *Angels With Dirty Faces*. He said, "I'll give you each $100 if you promise to be good." Mike loved us, he understood us. He was from the same background; he grew up in poverty in Hungary. There's no difference in Russia or America with poverty: you get a certain sense when you come out of it that you're an underdog.

We had a better system in Hollywood then. We've got good actors today, but the system is bad. The Dead End Kids were stars. But we were not under star contracts at Warner Bros., we were under player contracts. I could do a Dead End Kid picture and then do a bit in a Bogart picture. I don't think anybody at Warners — except James Cagney and Paul Muni — were *stars*. Everybody else was under a player contract, so they could put them anywhere. It was a great learning process.

Actors would help us. An actor would come and tell you — he wouldn't tell you, he would suggest to you. Today, I don't tell the kids. If they come and ask me, great. But I'm not about to tell 'em. That's what they don't have today — they don't have the comedy specialists working on the sets. They don't have the training ground today.

Shemp Howard taught me comedy; he was the first one who really took me by the hand. He taught us little tricks; most of the comics did. I love comics. I'd go on the set and watch Jimmy Durante, and I'd come back and start talking like him. "Were you on the Durante set?" "Yeah." No more. Or I'd watch W.C. Fields over at Universal. And I started to sound like him. I was mimicking them, without even realizing it.

When the Bowery Boys series ended, I went back to New York. I was 38 when my deal ended. It was difficult, but I had people who believed in me. There were people who said, "He's not a street punk, he's not the adolescent moron he played — he's an actor." I went back to the theatre, and the money wasn't important. Gabriel Dell went back and did theatre and he got a Tony nomination.

We proved we could act. We didn't let them put us in a category. It's that self-survival — it was in Mickey Rooney and Jackie Cooper; it's in Gabe Dell, it's in me. I don't think it was in Leo Gorcey. He became complacent; he just wanted to do the pictures and that was it. You can't stay in Hollywood and become oriented to pictures; you gotta go out and take a shot.

If you're not doing a TV series or a picture, it's death in Hollywood. I'd rather be in the theatre than do crap on TV. I run away from it. They think I'm nuts; they think I'm tempermental. But I don't want to do it. Theatre keeps me alive; it gives me a chance to show I'm an actor. In theatre they don't typecast you the way they do in motion pictures.

It's been [fifty] years since the original *Dead End* and the pictures are still going strong. It's unbelievable. The Bowery Boys were part of Americana. We were the first rebels. I don't think there are any messages; we weren't laying down anything. It was just knockout humor. There was no time element in the comedy.

A lot of people took from us — there's a lot of stuff out there that Leo Gorcey and I invented. Take *Happy Days* or *Welcome Back, Kotter* — they're rip-offs of the Bowery Boys. People are starting to laugh at pies in the face again. There's a time for humor, then it changes, then it comes back.

I love the Bowery Boys. If I put that down, I'm putting down my whole career. I wish everybody could have that success. It's stupid to resent it when you do something and the public loves you. If you resent it, you gotta hate yourself. The public loved me, and I'm not about to resent the public's love.

Everything around you can be bad, but if you knock yourself, you're in trouble. Negativity is the worst thing in the world. I don't accept "no." I turn it around and spell it backwards — it becomes "on." On to the next thing. On to the next job. I don't have time for "no."

Ray Johnson

On October 14, 1930, George and Ira Gershwin's Girl Crazy *premiered at the Alvin Theatre on Broadway. It featured two up-and-coming talents who were about to become famous: Ginger Rogers and Ethel Merman. But the most acclaimed cast members were a group of young men from the Pacific Northwest, who stopped the show with the opening number.*

The Foursome won rave reviews and became much in demand as a result of their appearance. "As for the strange quartette [sic] of gentlemen who roam on and off singing, 'I'm bidin' my time — that's the kind of guy I'm,' I want a whole show of them someday," observed The New Yorker *critic.*

J. Marshall Smith, first tenor, and L. Dwight Snyder, bass, hailed from Spokane, Washington, where they started singing together as schoolboys. Delmar S. Porter, second bass, and Raymond M. Johnson, baritone, both from the Portland area, met at Oregon State College.

The group began by playing one-night stands and singing background in Mack Sennett comedies. Their dismal New York debut in Ripples *was soon followed by the hit Gershwin show, after which they sang with Roger Wolfe Kahn (alias The Country Gentlemen) and traveled with Glenn Miller. They returned to Broadway in Cole Porter's* Anything Goes *(1934), which kept them busy for 66 weeks.*

The popular vocal quartet appeared in several films, including Born to Dance *with Eleanor Powell. They were featured regularly on* Kraft Music Hall *and recorded with Bing Crosby, Red Nichols, Ray Noble and other artists. Among their anonymous backup musicians was Spike Jones.*

The Foursome broke up late in 1941 when they were unable to replace Dwight Snyder, who was in failing health. Marshall Smith went into insurance; Ray Johnson switched to analytical chemistry. Del Porter had his own novelty band on the side, which evolved into the City Slickers when he went into partnership with Spike Jones.

Johnson, the quartet's arranger, is the last survivor of the Foursome today, the last one left to tell their story. Remarkably agile at 86, he lives in retirement in San Juan Capistrano, California, where he still dabbles in songwriting.

I met Del Porter in the early '20s. He played violin in a band that traveled around the country at that time, Stuffy McDaniels and his Bungalow Five. They were a great attraction. I was in Dwight Johnson's band, The Strollers; Del joined us in Portland. We were at the Davenport Hotel in Spokane for a year, and it was there we first met Bing Crosby. He was just a boy about town.

The Foursome quartet really began in 1928, at the Broadway Theatre in Portland. Jimmy Davis and I were with Georgie Stoll, Jim on guitar and I at the piano. These two kids came by — Marshall Smith and Dwight Snyder — they'd been with a quartet in the East that broke up. They were looking for two new members; they had connections. Davis and I quit our jobs at the Broadway and joined them.

We were on radio on Portland and an agent heard us; we hightailed it down to Los Angeles. Jim left us in San Francisco and that made us a trio. Del was working in Seattle; he had a good voice and was also an instrumentalist, which was a definite plus for us. He joined the quartet on clarinet.

After Del came in, we started to rehearse like crazy. We bought a Model T Ford for $25 — $6.25 apiece. Getting over the mountains to Los Angeles was a matter of pushing and riding, on and off, but we made it. Our agent booked us into one-nighters for a while; finally we got a job with Mack Sennett. Sound was just starting. We sang background in several comedies, then we did

Wild Party Girl with Clara Bow. Del and I wrote a song for the picture.

After that we got a 30-week contract with Paramount Publix Theatres. Those were the days when they had a revue that went along with the picture. We were in the "Rah Rah" unit. When we got back to New York we got a contract at New Amsterdam Theater for *Ripples* with Fred Stone. The music was written by Oscar Levant. It lasted four weeks. Then we were lucky; we got into *Girl Crazy* and it was a smash.

We didn't like our song in the show — "Bidin' My Time" — but that was the greatest thing for us. We were surprised people went for it. Musicians still talk about the pit band in *Girl Crazy*: Gene Krupa on drums; Jimmy Dorsey and Benny Goodman on sax; Glenn Miller on trombone; Charlie Teagarden on trumpet. Red Nichols was the bandleader. Imagine them in the pit, playing for the dancing girls.

In 1933 Smith Ballew and Glenn Miller formed a band and we went on the road with them. The first job we had was at a society dance in Philadelphia. The next day we played a job in Pottstown. Smith and Glenn could put the liquor away pretty good; they came in about an hour and a half late, hardly in any condition to be playing. The manager started giving Glenn what for — and Miller, when he had a few drinks, you didn't mess with him. He said something to Glenn that Glenn didn't like. Glenn reached over and grabbed Del's clarinet and told the manager to get off the stage or, he said, "I'm going to run this right through your stomach." We played the rest of the date that night, and we never got paid for it.

When we found out the producers of *Girl Crazy* were going to do *Anything Goes* we went to see them and got a spot in the show, a musical with Ethel Merman. In this show we sang a sea chanty written for us by Cole Porter. It ran for a year in New York and then we went on tour.

Ray Johnson, bottom left, with Del Porter (tin whistle), Dwight Snyder and Marshall Smith, 1934. Note the unique gourd-shaped ocarinas or "sweet potatoes" played by the quartet.

We came out to Los Angeles and signed a contract to appear in *Born to Dance* at MGM. We were supposed to go back to New York but we stayed. Bing Crosby, our friend from Spokane, was the star of *Kraft Music Hall* at this time, about 1937. Bing asked us to come on and do a guest spot once in a while. Every summer when he went on vacation we'd take over; we were on every week with Bob "Bazooka" Burns.

The Foursome made a lot of Decca records, several with Crosby. "El Rancho Grande" was a big hit for Bing, and we were on that; Del and I wrote one for Bing called "Poor Old Rover." We also entertained at the rather unusual premiere of Bing's movie, *Pennies From Heaven*. It was held at the Del Mar racetrack. The screen replaced the pari-mutuel facilities and the audience sat in the grandstand.

We had a background unit that was with us all the time: Perry Botkin on guitar, Jack Mayhew on sax, Slim Taft on bass and Spike Jones on drums. Spike changed a lot. When he was one of the support members of our group, he was glad to get a job. After that, I hardly knew him — he hardly knew me. But he did record a song Del and I wrote called "My Pretty Girl." Del and I wrote songs together before the Foursome; this was the only one that amounted to anything. Lawrence Welk and others recorded it too.

The Foursome made a couple of records with Red Nichols, and one called "Home Cookin'" with Bob Hope and Margaret Whiting. Then we signed for Kellogg's *Circle Hour* over NBC radio. We were guest artists on that three months. Then Kellogg did not pick up the option on the show, due to war clouds appearing in the Pacific sector. That was in December 1941 — and that was when we broke up.

George Rock

The mainstay of Spike Jones' musical disorganization from 1944 to 1960 was the aptly-named George Rock, a 6 ft. 250 lb. trumpet player with a talent to match his size. His roommate, Del Porter of the Foursome — who had exerted great influence over Jones in the early '40s — felt Rock "spoiled the flavor of the band... because he played so many notes." But Spike found him indispensable. And Rock, moreso than any one else, became responsible for the inimitable sound of the City Slickers during their heyday.

"Spike could hire all the trumpet players he wanted, but none of them could play like George," says Jones' longtime staffwriter Eddie Brandt. "George was the only one you couldn't do a show without. We could not have played without him." Rock increased his value to the band by augmenting his virtuoso trumpet solos with oral sound effects — cackles, belchs, razzberries — and comic vocals; his high-pitched child's voice sold over two million copies of "All I Want for Christmas is My Two Front Teeth."

George David Rock was born October 11, 1919, in Farmer City, Illinois. He attended the Wesleyan School of Music before turning professional at 20. After touring with various bands and working in a St. Joseph, Missouri gambling club, he joined Freddie Fisher's popular Schnickelfritz Band. With Fisher he played Gene Austin's Hollywood night club, the Blue Heaven, and made a number of radio and movie appearances, including The Farmer's Daughter.

Rock then worked briefly with Charlie Barnet and Mike Riley, joining Spike Jones immediately after the City Slickers' 1944 USO tour. He quickly became the star of the troupe, playing trumpet for Jones' RCA Victor records (beginning with "Cocktails for Two"), network radio and TV shows, movies (notably Ladies' Man *and* Fireman, Save My

Child) *and* Musical Depreciation Revue, *a two-hour extravaganza that resembled a traveling circus.*

In addition to "Two Front Teeth," his little-boy voice was heard on such popular novelty records as "Blowing Bubble Gum" (which he performed for President Truman at a 1948 dinner party) and "Ya Wanna Buy a Bunny?" — which has since become one of the staples of Dr. Demento's nationally-syndicated radio program.

Rock left Jones in 1960 to play the Las Vegas-Reno-Lake Tahoe circuit with his own sextet. After working with San Francisco jazz legend Turk Murphy, he returned to Lake Tahoe with a quartet and later recorded an album with fellow Slicker alumnus Joe Siracusa ("The New Society Band Shoves It in Your Ear").

I started on the horn when I was 14 or 15. The whole family was musically inclined, but not professional. The only time I ever practiced my horn was when my father would try to get me to go out and mow the yard or something. That was my standard excuse — I couldn't because I had to work on the horn.

I started professionally around 1939. A band came through my home town; they were to play the fair. They were rained out the first night. They met at a local hang out downtown and had a semi-jam session. I was the local musical hero so they all insisted I go home and get my horn. I came down and sat in with this band and they offered me a job. It was kind of a starvation job, but I got my foot in the door and got out of Farmer City.

Around 1942 I went with Freddie Fisher, and that's how I ended up in Hollywood. It really was kind of a forerunner of Spike's band. He had a washboard and all the tuned automobile horns. We played a semi-dixieland type music but a lot of novelty songs. Fisher existed long before Spike started his band; Spike probably was influenced by Freddie and I think both of them maybe by the Hoosier Hot Shots.

Spike gave me a seven-year contract, and after the first couple weeks he tore up the contract and doubled my salary. First I got

$200 a week, then it went up to $400. He was always very good to me in that respect; I didn't have to ask for anything. He really paid me for my efforts.

The stage show was hard work, and lots of times you didn't feel like doing it. You'd have the flu or something and nobody cared; you still had to come out and do the show. When my father died I wasn't able to go home because I had to stay with the band. They couldn't call and have someone come in and play my part while I was gone.

The shows were all strictly routine. Everything was done as per rehearsal. Spike had a washtub full of cowbells on stage, and he'd pick it up and dump 'em out. One time the guys nailed it to the floor. He almost got a hernia trying to lift the tub up off the floor. You had to do things like that to keep from going crazy. Doodles Weaver did a lot of strange things. He had a picture of Christ above his bed that said, "To Doodles, from J.C."

Our writers traveled with us constantly. A few times Spike asked me to sit in on the writing sessions; I hated it. I honestly tried to do things to get out of it, and sure enough, pretty soon I wasn't asked. They would go all night. We would work until 11 p.m. or midnight, and then these guys would go until 4 o'clock in the morning on the writing session. I didn't want any of that.

Spike hired me for my musical ability, rather than any comedy talent or vocals. I don't think he really knew about that too much until I'd joined him. We were getting ready to do some recording at RCA and Spike asked what all I could do. I did a couple of the voices I had done for Freddie Fisher, and he was enthralled with the little [child] voice and wanted to put something in the stage show, which we did.

When we played theatres [vaudeville] I did "I Want to Get Married," the trumpet number "Minka" and a short little thing on "Mairzy Dotes." I sang, "Mairzy [razzberry] Dotes [razzberry] and little lambs that [razzberry] ..." We'd occasionally get a few objections to that, the straight-laced people in Boston.

The recording sessions were pretty cut and dried. The only one I remember that was different — we'd had a party at Spike's house and we were to go down to RCA and record "Hawaiian War Chant" after the party. Everybody was... not everybody, but there were enough of us stoned that we couldn't get it recorded; We had to call off the session and come back the next morning.

There was a record ban [due] at the end of 1947, so we recorded basically everything we could get our hands on. Somebody in the group saw a song called "Two Front Teeth" laying on the piano. They picked it up and said, "Let's give it a shot." We never did rehearse it. We just picked it up and recorded it.

"I Saw Mommy Kissing Santa Claus" was the next year after "Two Front Teeth." We recorded all the background with the choir and everything, then they were excused; the choir went home and we did [the song] with dirty lyrics. It seemed like a good idea, I suppose. Spike didn't want anybody to hear it; the public was never allowed to hear it.

Spike was always very strict in adhering to the fact that this was a family-type show, and nothing would be done that would offend anybody. Closest he ever came was that "Mairzy Dotes" thing I did. For some reason he didn't think that should be offensive to anybody, and staunchly defended it.

They gave me a bonus for "Two Front Teeth" and royalties after that. They thought I was going to leave, I guess, and the manager came to me and said, "If anybody makes an offer, give us a chance to better it." Damn fool, I should've gone and told him about all the big offers I was getting.

I missed not being able to be with my family, not being with my kids as they grew up. I didn't think about it so much at the time, because I figured it was a good living for them and I was able to give them everything they needed. Later, in retrospect, you try to balance it and see if it was worth it. We always had quite a bit of time at home, but it didn't really justify the other times when we were gone.

George Rock died April 12, 1988, in Champaign, Illinois, after a long battle with diabetes. He was 68 years old.

TRADITIONAL MUSIC

Eubie Blake

Buckdancer, vaudevillian and showman, arranger, composer and concert artist, Eubie Blake was living proof until the end of his remarkable life that youth is not necessarily wasted on the young.

The legendary James Hubert Blake was born February 7, 1883, on his father's 50th birthday. His career took him from the sporting houses of his native Baltimore, where he began playing at 15, to the White House. He composed his first song, "The Charleston Rag," in 1899, the same year Scott Joplin introduced the classic "Maple Leaf Rag."

In 1921 Blake and partner Noble Sissle created the first all-black Broadway musical, Shuffle Along, in collaboration with the comedy team of Flournoy Miller and Aubrey Lyles. Subsequent shows included The Chocolate Dandies, Blackbirds of 1930 and Tan Manhattan.

Blake composed over 1,000 songs, including "I'm Just Wild About Harry," "Love Will Find a Way," "Memories of You," "Low Down Blues, "I'm Just Simply Full of Jazz," "You Got to Git the Gittin While the Gittin's Good," "Bandana Days" and "Oriental Blues."

In the '70s, his hit songs were revived in Bubbling Brown Sugar and showcased in Eubie! His music more popular than ever, the elder statesman of ragtime found himself in constant demand in later years. At 89, he started his own record company; at 90, he appeared with the Boston Pops. He was a youngster of 93 when he played the proprietor of the Maple Leaf Club in a TV movie about Scott Joplin.

How did he keep going? What was the secret of his longevity? "I don't know. I'm just a man, same as any other," he said modestly, during an interview in Beverly Hills, California. "You have to fight the mental conditioning, I guess. You can't look at that number — 96 — and say, 'Well, I guess I'm through.'" Blake, who was visiting the West Coast in conjunction with the tour of Eubie!, remained alert throughout the lengthy late night conversation; the publicist, a man half his age, dozed off mid-way through the evening.

I started when I was four years old. I went shopping one night with my mother. She looked around and didn't see me. She screamed, "Where's my boy?" I heard somebody playing the organ, and I went across the street. They didn't have automobiles then; there was no traffic.

This man was demonstrating an organ, the kind you peddle with your feet. I went to this organ and got up on the bench and started foolin' around. I saw the manager play, and I did the same thing with all my fingers, but it wouldn't play because I wasn't pumpin'. I couldn't reach the pedals. The manager said, "He's a genius!" My mother said, "I don't care what kind of genius he is, I don't want him bein' no pianna plunker." Until the day she died, she said, "You ain't gonna be nuthin' but a pianna plunker."

I was about six years old when I took piano lessions from the next-door neighbor. One day I was playing my lesson... I didn't like it. When my mother wasn't in the house, I jazzed it up. One day I'm playin', I don't know what she was doin' home that time of day, but I turned around and there she was. "Take that ragtime out of my house. As long as you live, don't you play no ragtime in this house."

I was about 12 when I first heard it. A big-time Negro would die, and the street band would play Chopin. I'd be sittin' out, and I'd hear 'em comin'. My mother'd say, "Don't you follow that band." "No ma'am." It'd be about four blocks away and I'd say, "Mamma, can I go out and play?" "Yes, but don't follow that band." Then I'd run up the hill and follow the band, all the way to the cemetary. Goin' up to the cemetery they'd play the funeral march; coming back, they'd play the same thing, but they jazzed it up.

Ragtime is nuthin' but syncopation. Take "Waltz of the Flowers" by my favorite composer, Tchaikovsky — that's not ragtime. But as soon as you syncopate it, *that's* ragtime! You got to swing the bass. The average ragtime piano player today doesn't

Blake at the piano, with vaudeville partner and song collaborator Noble Sissle, circa 1920.

play bass, he plays chords. The world is sittin' on a base; they call it an axis. When you take that away, you're taking away the foundation. Disco, rock 'n' roll — I don't knock it, but there's no bass. And the discos are packed. But you can't knock a success — I don't care how lousy it is.

I played in the hookshops. I started off big — Aggie Shelton's — it was a $5 house. My mother and father, they worked so hard they died every night. They didn't go to sleep, they *died*. When I heard the old man put that boot down, I'd get up and sneak out of the house. I'd go over to the pool room on the corner and give the guy 25 cents for a pair of long pants. Aggie Shelton guaranteed me $3 a night, if I didn't make that much in tips. She never paid me the first dime. I got $5, $10; I got as much as $20 for playing one tune. And I knew all the tunes.

Then one of the sisters of the church told my mother, "I

heard little Hubie playing in Aggie Shelton's." "What time was it?" "One a.m." "Oh, no, that boy goes to bed at nine." Which I did. But when the preacher's wife came — she can't lie. "Sister Blake, I heard little Hubie playing in Aggie Shelton's." "How do you know it's Hubie?" "He 's the only one who plays that wobble-wobble bass. There ain't no one else plays that way." Which there wasn't — I created that myself.

When my mother was mad at me, she called me "Mr. Blake." I came downstairs. "Mr. Blake!" "Yes, ma'am." "You playin' in a place called Aggie Shelton's?" "Well-uh-uh..." "Don't you lie to me. You playin' in that bawdy house?" My father comes home. He knows Aggie Shelton's is a hookshop — a $5 house, not one of them tap-on-the-window-come-on-in places. "You playin' in that place?" "Yes, sir." "How much you gettin'?" He made $9 a week 'cause he was boss of the stevedores.

We didn't have no carpet. I pulled up the oil cloth and showed him all the money I made in tips. "You steal that money, boy?" "No, sir. I play and the white folks give it to me." He saw $5, he changed. He knows he's going to get some of that. "Well, I'll talk to your mother."

I didn't write "The Charleston Rag," I composed it. The lady who taught me how to read music, I don't know if she could write music. I didn't learn to write until 1915. Songwriters and composers are different things. I don't like nobody to call me a songwriter; I'm a composer. Those other fellows, they went to school to learn how to write; I never studied it.

Noble Sissle and I wrote a song called "It's All Your Fault." Sophie Tucker was just beginning to be a big star. Sissle said, "Miss Tucker's playing at the Maryland Theatre. Let's go see her." I said, "Are you crazy? We can't see her." "She can't kill us." Sissle always had that and I didn't — "Now Eubie, don't you meddle in the white folks' business" — that's the way I was brought up. He was raised different.

You couldn't go anywhere near Sophie Tucker her first performance; she would get stage fright. She took three bows, came off. "Miss Tucker?" "Yes? Yes?" "We have a song I'd like you to hear." "You've got a song for me?" Sissle sang it for her. "I'll take it." It was a sensation the way she did it. But you know how far the first song of ours went? Annapolis is 20 miles from Baltimore, and nobody in Annapolis ever heard of it.

There was a guy named Leslie Stuart; I liked his style. He wrote "Floradora." This was 1900. And I wrote this waltz, "I'm Just Wild About Harry." Twenty-one years later, we were putting on *Shuffle Along*. We brought Lottie Gee over from London for the show. I played the song for her; she said, "It's a beautiful song but I can't sing it." "Why not?" She said, "Who ever heard of a waltz in a colored show?" I said, "I did."

Lottie said, "If you put it in one-step I'll be glad to sing it." I said, "I'm not going to change it." Sissle said, "Yes, you are. You're going to change it right now."

I think "Weary" is my best song. It's a Negroid lament, speaking of the tribulations of the slaves. Andy Razaf wrote the lyric. "Memories of You" is another one. I like melody. I was taught to write for the human voice; I don't write for piano.

They had a meeting in Washington, and I was invited. They had all these big-time lawyers. I was the last man that spoke. I said, "Gentlemen, I feel like a fly in a pan of milk" — I only went through the fifth grade. I said, "The record companies pay us two cents a record. I can't tell you what to do — I'm not a businessman — but I got sense enough to know they should pay us more than two cents." You should have heard the applause; I thought the house would come down.

Eubie Blake died of pneumonia at his home in Brooklyn, New York, on February 12, 1983, just five days after his 100th birthday.

Jester Hairston

As the name Eubie Blake is now synonymous with ragtime, choral conductor and arranger Jester Hairston — Blake's one-time teacher and lifelong admirer — is identified with the Negro spiritual throughout the world. He is perhaps best known for his composition, "Amen," which he dubbed for Sidney Poitier in the film Lilies of the Field.

Jester Hairston was born in Blews Creek, North Carolina on July 9, 1901. He grew up in the little steel mill town of Homestead, Pennsylvania; his father, who worked in the coke ovens, died when he was less than two.

At the University of Massachusetts, he was quarterback on the football team. He dropped out due to lack of funds and worked in the steel mills before resuming his education; in 1929 he graduated cum laude from Tufts University, and went to New York with the intention of setting up a concert tour. He sang with Eva Jessye before joining the famed Hall Johnson Choir, becoming assistant conductor under Johnson in 1933.

Hairston came to Hollywood with the choir to do the music for the film Green Pastures *and stayed to work on the Academy Award-winning score for* Lost Horizon, *with Dimitri Tiomkin. He became and remained Tiomkin's choral arranger for 20 years, contributing to the scores for* Duel in the Sun, Red River, She Wore a Yellow Ribbon *and other films. To take up the slack between choral jobs, he did extra work in Tarzan movies and pictures like* The Road to Morocco.

During World War II, he traveled to Europe with a USO tour of Shuffle Along, *entertaining soldiers in Italy and Germany. In 1949 he was working with the Walter Schumann Choir in Hollywood when a visitor invited him to the College of the Pacific to teach Negro spirituals. The response prompted Schumann to publish Hairston's arrangements, and he soon found himself in demand at high schools and colleges throughout the United States.*

The State Department began sending Dr. Hairston overseas as a goodwill ambassador in 1960. Meanwhile, his stock as an actor rose with a dual role on Amos 'n' Andy *and a featured part in* The Alamo, *as Richard Widmark's slave. He has since appeared in* To Kill a Mockingbird, Lady Sings the Blues *and other films; on TV, he had the recurring role of Wildcat in* That's My Mama *and is currently seen as Deacon Rolly Forbes in* Amen.

If heart trouble and arthritis have slowed his pace in recent years, he has remarkable energy for a man of 86. Moreover, Jester has a manner and a disposition that seems to endear him to everyone he meets. "Making friends all over the world and trying to make brothers of us all, that's the only way I believe we are going to get along," he says.

I studied agriculture at the University of Massachusetts. I sang in the glee club just for fun. A woman took an interest in my voice and began to teach me songs; she was the one who persuaded me that I had talent, to go into singing as a profession. I was going to be a landscape designer, but this woman kept nagging me until finally she got me to thinking that I could sing.

The first big show I auditioned for was *Hello Paris* with Chic Sale. A little man came out and said, "Gentlemen, I have all the Negroes I need except two low basses and a second tenor." I was a low baritone; I couldn't compete with the basses so I told the man I was a tenor. I did a little ditty for him and then he took me aside.

He said, "You've got a job. We'll use you in the show." I said, "Oh, thank you." He said, "But not as a singer, because you can't sing." I said, "I'm the best baritone in Boston." He said, "Don't get excited, son, this is New York. You can sing in a Baptist church in Boston, but not on Broadway; you can't compete. These men can all sing, but not one of them can read. I'm going to have you help these men learn the music of the show."

Hairston (right), with members of the Hall Johnson Choir in the show, *Run Little Chillun*; with Richard Widmark in *The Alamo* (1960).

As Henry Van Porter (bottom right), in *Amos 'n' Andy*. Clockwise, from bottom: Nick Stewart, Alvin Childress, Johnny Lee, Tim Moore, Spencer Williams and Ernestine Wade.

Hairston at the piano, in his Los Angeles home.

He also gave me some advice. He said, "Jester, don't try to compete as a singer. You'll never make it. You want to be in the theatre? Become an arranger, or a conductor, and teach other people how to sing. Twenty-five years from now, most of these men will be retired; their voices will be gone. But you, as a conductor — you can last 50 years." And I have.

I didn't take conducting formally in school; I studied with Hall Johnson and watched his movements. When I first joined his choir I wasn't too happy with the music; they were singing only Negro spirituals and I thought it was a waste of time. In Boston I'd been singing the classics, and all that stuff.

The spirituals didn't mean anything to me then. Those old church songs, Good Lord! That dialect was beneath me; I wanted to get away from that. Then here came Hall Johnson, singing these songs with this dialect, and the people loved it — intelligent people in white audiences. I said, "Well, there must be something about these songs." I began to go to the library and read about black history, and I began to get the feel that the music was worthwhile.

My life is devoted now to keeping the spirituals alive, because even the blacks are letting them die — they're going into gospel music, writing for money. But these songs were written by my ancestors, who were slaves.

One evening Marc Connelly and Mike Todd came to see Johnson, to discuss a new show called *Green Pastures*. We figured it was just another one of those colored shows. Hall couldn't use me as a conductor; he told me I could sing in the choir and they'd pay me $40 a week. I was living with a doctor; music was his hobby. He said, "A graduate of Tufts working for $40 a week? What do they think you are, a pauper? Tell 'em to go to hell, Jester." So I told Johnson I couldn't work for $40 a week. The show ran for three years, and I was broke.

Warner Bros. bought the show at the end of its Broadway run and brought us out to Hollywood to do the music for the film.

I was the assistant conductor of the choir. In one scene De Lawd was coming through heaven and I offered to sell him a five-cent cigar; that was my film debut.

After *Green Pastures* we did the music for other pictures. Dimitri Tiomkin wanted the Hall Johnson Choir for *Lost Horizon*, but he had to fight for us — the studio said, "Whoever heard of niggers singing Russian music?" But he said, "I don't see colors, I hear sounds."

When Hall went back to New York I got a mixed choir — I knew I couldn't survive with just a black one because they called a black choir only when they had cotton-picking music to do. I got two-thirds white singers and one-third black, and I had a heck of a time. But Dimitri called me in on a picture and said, "Bring me the best in Hollywood." I brought this mixed group in and he was tickled to death. When the studios found out I could please the greatest composer in town, they began to call me for other pictures.

When I couldn't find any singing jobs, I applied at the studios for acting parts. They said, "No, you're a conductor. We've got good actors." They always put you in the category that they first see you in. No casting director would give me a job, so I worked as an extra. All the Tarzan pictures with Johnny Weissmuller — I'm in there as a native, running around naked with rings in my nose and a spear, yelling "Bwana" this, "Bwana" that. Finally I got promoted; I got a job as a witch doctor in *Tarzan's Hidden Jungle* with Gordon Scott.

Ernestine Wade, who'd been singing with me, told me they were auditioning for the part of Leroy, the Kingfish's brother-in-law, on *Amos 'n' Andy*. Then they created Henry Van Porter, a very proper man; I was Porter in one scene and Leroy in another; I did it on radio and television for 16 years.

You had to do the stereotypes then. If it hadn't been for Stepin Fetchit, you wouldn't have had Sidney Poitier and Harry Belafonte. And you wouldn't have had Fetchit if it hadn't been for the minstrels.

Minstrels were the first real American entertainment. White men came down from the theatre in New York and visited the plantation; they saw these slaves singing and dancing and they went back and started minstrels, with the whites blacking their faces. When slavery was over the blacks started their own minstrel companies; they blacked their faces, imitating the whites imitating them. Then we were stereotyped because the first thing the whites saw us doing was shuffling our feet and cracking these "coon jokes." That stigma has stayed with us all through the theatre and it's still on us.

I don't encounter prejudice at all now. Some years ago when I was conducting the Mormon Tabernacle Choir, I was having lunch in a restaurant. A man asked me if I lived there and I told him no, I was working at the Tabernacle. He was a Mormon evidently, and he was visibly shaken by my remark. We continued talking, and he looked at me and said, "Mister, do you know you the first Oriental that ever conducted in the Tabernacle?"

I said, "Oriental?" He said, "Yes, you've got to be Oriental; they wouldn't let a black conduct in the Tabernacle." That night I called my wife; she was born in Salt Lake City and she knew the prejudice there. She said, "How are you doing in my home town?" I said, "I'm passing for Chinese up here and doing fine."

Mickey Katz

If comedians make no apologies for being Jewish today, they were not always so forthright about it. Long before Woody Allen and Mel Brooks showered moviegoers with Yiddish slang, a little clarinetist with a lot of chutzpah blazed the trail, exposing "crossover" audiences to the language with a series of English-Yiddish parody records.

Being Jewish *"was always popular in my house,"* said Mickey Katz, *who embraced his heritage from the outset of his career. "The only people it wasn't popular with were those who were frightened." Among those who tried to stifle him was the Jewish editor of* Variety, *who took him to task for "defiling" the legend of Davy Crockett when the bandleader's parody "Duvid Crockett" sold 200,000 records.*

Meyer Myron Katz was born in Cleveland, June 15, 1909. He toured with Phil Spitalny when he was 17, and later worked with Maurice Spitalny at Cleveland's RKO Palace Theatre. Following a USO tour and a stint with Spike Jones (he provided the throat "glugs" for live renditions of "Cocktails for Two"), he put together a group of musicians called the Kosher Jammers. The band, which included trumpeter Mannie Klein, drummer Sammy Weiss and the legendary Ziggy Elman, specialized in comedy and klezmer — *a raucous Old World jazz with roots in the folk music of Eastern Europe.*

*Recording first for RCA Victor and then for Capitol, Katz produced such popular parody records as "Borscht Riders in the Sky," "That's Morris" and "Yiddish Mule Train," and toured with a hit variety show (*Borscht Capades*) that introduced his son, Joel Grey. Hello, Solly, a 1967 revue, landed Katz on Broadway while Grey was appearing in* Cabaret, *which won his son the Tony award.*

The entertainer toured England, Australia and South Africa during the course of his career, but found his warmest reception on the Flor-

ida "condo circuit" in his later years. "The condominiums are the greatest audiences in the world," Katz observed in an interview at the Friars Club in Beverly Hills, California. "They come for the comedy but when we play a little jazz they go crazy. I tell 'em stories, sing a few songs, play some Jewish folk music — whatever's necessary to make 'em happy."

My father was a tremendous music lover, even though he was a poor tailor. He'd sit on top of the opera house for half a buck to listen to an opera. My sister was a piano player, my other sister was a singer and my brother was a violinist. At the age of 11 I felt I wasn't doing anything; I was left out. I said, "Pa, I want to play something too. I want to be a musician."

There was a concert at the Talmud Torah, the Hebrew school, in the middle of the old Jewish neighborhood in Cleveland. I went down and a boy of 14 played on the clarinet the "Shadow Song" from *Dinorah.* And I said, "Papa, that's the one I want to play." But my parents were desperately poor; they didn't have anything. They did have *one* thing — there was a lot of love in the family.

Half a year later I went to Central Jr. High School. They applied to the Board of Education for a free instrument that they gave to needy youngsters. And the clarinet that I got was marked "U.S. Army, 1898." It was left over from the Spanish American War!

I was a gutsy little guy. Within two months of when I started taking lessons, I started playing amateur nights. There were theatres that gave away prizes, either $5 or $4 or a box of candy. I went in the first time and I started playing "St. Louis Blues" and I was shakin' my little torso around pretty good, and I won first prize. Then my sister got into these things. Many a night we were together on the same bill and we'd divide the prize. One night all we won was a five-pound box of candy; we went outside and sold it for $2.

106

Down on the Bar Mitzvah Ranch, in a moment from *Borscht Capades.*

In 1928 — right out of high school — I was working with Doc Whipple's band at the Golden Pheasant Chinese Restaurant in Cleveland. They had three sessions a day — noon to 2 p.m., 6 to 8 and 10 to 1 a.m. It was a murderously tough job. I used to write a lot of poetry, and at that time I was writing parodies like "Little Red Rosenberg" and "General Huckster's Last Stand." They had a radio pickup and I got a chance to do these things there. It was a good 20 years later that I started recording the song parodies.

I worked with Jean Harlow when I was playing at the RKO Palace Theatre in Cleveland. Whenever any show came along that would need a gagster out of the band, it would always be me. Harlow's straight man, Nils Granulund, told me at rehearsal I had to be in long underwear — which, living in Cleveland, everybody owned — and I had a little derby. Everybody knew me because I played clarinet solos in the pit. Nils put me in the closet. He said, "This is the bit — I come home late from work and she says, 'Hello, darling.'" And at that point the drummer would make a scratching sound on his snare drum. Nils says, "It sounds like there's a rat somewhere" — and I'd push open the door and say, "Who's a rrrrrrat?"

I wrote a lot of things for Spike Jones and I used to conduct the shows for him. He was a big attraction. Once we came into Mason City, Iowa, in the middle of a flood. They took us off the train in boats and we went to play a mile or two away where it was raining and flooding pretty badly, and there were 3,000 people waiting for us.

Spike Jones didn't pay big money, because he didn't have to. Everybody wanted to play with his band. We knocked our fucking brains out in Washington, D.C., doing six shows a day. Spike said, "You'll all get a big bonus for this." You know what we got? We each got an $18.75 war bond. He made $80,000 that week.

I left Spike finally because I was on long extended tours like 100 nights on the road and I thought I'd better get home and see my children grow a little more. I got home and I went to RCA where Spike did his recordings; I had a good friend there and I told him I had a couple of parodies I'd like to record. One was "Haim afen Range" ("Home on the Range") and the other was "The Yiddish Square Dance."

After the record was out about 10 days, my friend at RCA called me up. He said, "They're selling about 5,000 copies a day of this record in New York." I had no idea it would get that kind of response.

But there were many, many people who were frightened — frightened of everything. If you said a Jewish word they'd start crawling in the backyard for fear that somebody was around the corner. I didn't pay any attention to those people. All the words I was using were really very innocent; they were words I heard at home. You know what made it popular? Those kids in Israel. They weren't afraid of anything; they were willing to stand up for what they were.

Allan Sherman came out with a record and sold a million copies. But by that time I'd softened things up a bit. It was much tougher for me. I had to do it first, then it was easy. But I must say, whatever he did was wonderful.

Everybody knew when they made a record there'd be a Mickey Katz record to follow. And the publishers were tickled. They were the ones that got the money — I never got paid for my lyrics. The original lyricist had to be paid. They were in great shape; they didn't care what I did with their songs.

Some of our non-Jewish audiences were more interested in the music than they were in the lyrics. They went crazy for the music. I had a song called "Herring Boats" that was mostly in Yiddish that sold 350,000 copies, of which 80,000 were sold in Louisiana. Just the fact that there was the sound of a horn of a guy selling fish down there, they bought it. And they liked the music. So how do you figure it?

After I'd made some records a fellow named Hal Zeiger whom I'd known back in Cleveland said, "We ought to put on a show." I knew there was a new generation of American Jewish people who didn't understand the old Jewish theatre because it was all in Yiddish. So I put on a Catskill-type revue called *Borscht Capades.*

Joel was a tremendous asset to the show. People love seeing a youngster. He started out with us at the Wilshire Ebell Theatre in Los Angeles — that was his first performance, with us on stage as a singer and dancer. He was a natural.

A woman came up to me after I played a condominium concert for about 1,900 people. She said, "Excuse me, Mr. Katz, is your son Joel Grey?" I said, "Yes." She said, "What was his name before it was Grey?" I said, "Katz." She said, "You know, I thought so."

I've satisfied myself as a musician; I've played with all the best musicians in the world. The audiences I've met are wonderful. And there's the fact that I came from the beautiful family that I did, with a father and mother who were the essence of *Yiddishkeit,* of family love — which I've transmitted to my family. We all hang on each other with love and adulation.

Mickey Katz died of kidney failure at his home in West Los Angeles on April 30, 1985, age 75. His granddaughter, Jennifer Grey, has since emerged as a star with the film, Dirty Dancing.

GOLDEN GIRLS

Laura La Plante

Laura La Plante is best remembered for her light comedy roles in silent pictures like Skinner's Dress Suit *with Reginald Denny, and the 1927 "old dark house" classic,* The Cat and the Canary, *which is still revived at Halloween. Unlike many stars of the movies' early days, her "girl next door" image was not a manufactured one.*

Laura La Plante was born in St. Louis, November 1, 1904. She was a naïve schoolgirl when she made her movie debut as an extra in 1918. Twelve years later she was earning $3500 at Universal when she quit because "I just didn't want to work any more. I didn't really walk out on my contract [as reported], I just got tired."

Among her silent and early sound films were The Old Swimmin' Hole *with Charles Ray,* Sporting Youth, Poker Faces, Finders Keepers *and* The King of Jazz. *She departed from her wholesome blonde look as the brunette Magnolia in the 1929 film version of* Show Boat.

After leaving Universal, she divorced her first husband, director William Seiter, and in 1934 married producer Irving Asher. They made their home for several years in London, where La Plante kept busy with stage and film work until she retired to raise a family.

She returned to the stage in 1956 to "redeem myself," appearing in a series of stage vehicles with Edward Everett Horton, including The White Sheep of the Family *and his oft-revived* Springtime for Henry. *On screen, she played Betty Hutton's mother in* Spring Reunion, *prompting more than one observer to remark that she looked "too young" for the role.*

Shortly after Laura La Plante was interviewed at her home in Rancho Mirage, California, she was spotlighted in a Life *magazine feature on former screen stars. She was not happy with the result: "It didn't occur to me that they were going to use a picture of you as you were in your youth, and a big color one of you as you are now. I wouldn't have been caught dead in that photograph if I could have avoided it."*

My family came from Missouri. I was going to school in San Diego, California, and I had a cousin in Hollywood, so I came up for the school holidays. I was not quite 14. My cousin saw an ad in the paper for children to be in a crowd scene in a film, so I went down and I was in that.

Later my cousin moved to a house near Gower Gulch, around the corner from Christie Studios. She said, "Just walk down there and ask them if they need anybody." So I went down to the studio offices and I saw a woman in a little cubbyhole. I said, "I came to see if anybody needed anybody in a film." A man came running out and said one of the bridesmaids didn't show up for a wedding scene.

He sent me over to wardrobe and told them to put my hair up, to make me look more grown up; I was still only 14. I didn't know anything. I didn't even know where the camera was — the first thing I did was walk right through the background of a shot while they were filming.

I worked two or three days on the first picture there, at $5 a day. I kept going down to the studio and they put me in things. One day I saw Al Christie talking to a carpenter and I went over and said, "Hey, how do you get in stock around here?" He said, "From now on, you're in it — Monday through Friday." In stock I was guaranteed five days a week.

Al Christie was often down on the set, to see how things were going. One time he went over to Dorothy Devore and put his arm around her and gave her a tight squeeze and whispered something in her ear. I thought that was absolutely lewd; I thought Christie Studios was really a den of iniquity. But he was just giving her a friendly hug.

I was The Baby at Christie. Al called me that and then the others. We used to put on our own makeup there — it was long before they had any rules about that, or about children working in films or anything. I think I got an agent while I was there. I

114

Seeking protection from the equally timid Creighton Hale in *The Cat and the Canary* (1927).

At home in Palm Desert, with one of her sculptures.

photo by the author

didn't think about being a star; I wasn't starstruck or anything, but I was usually by the camera watching other people's scenes.

I felt I was doing satisfactory as long as they didn't throw me out. Eventually, I began to get a little confidence in myself; I was getting the approval of others. I started getting interested in getting better parts; I figured it was a better way to make a living than working in a department store, and it was more fun.

Christie specialized in domestic comedies. They didn't do any slapstick. Their two-reelers were quality films; they were the elite of that type of comedy. The films were broad, but not nearly as crude as Mack Sennett Comedies. They used to have the men do a "double wings" where they'd fall down, jump up and kick their legs out — they'd say, "Do a double wings and scram."

What was special about the silent films was the pantomime. You had to get over the story without words. The scripts actually had dialogue in those days. We didn't learn the lines but we got over the idea. The director gave us the situation, who said what to who, and we pretty much conveyed it.

After Christie I did two-reel westerns over at Universal. Then I was signed to a five-year contract there. I was absolutely thrilled to come home and tell the family I was making $250 a week. I got up as high as $3500 a week at Universal. The idea that anybody would pay me that much was paralyzing. I didn't have anything to say about what films I did, or script approval — I was being paid, and I did what they told me.

Irving Thalberg, who was Carl Laemmle's secretary at Universal, was the one who suggested they sign me. Later when he went to Metro-Goldwyn-Mayer he wanted me to go with him. I said I was under contract, and he said, "We'll fix that." I didn't know he was going to buy out the contract. I didn't know anything about that; I thought it was something crooked.

MGM knew how to develop their people. They wanted to develop me into a big star. You were yourself at Universal; there was no encouragement to develop as an actress, to take singing or dancing lessons or anything. I'm sorry I misunderstood Thalberg. That's one of my regrets. But I felt I was honorbound; I thought he was asking me to do something shady. Talk about the age of innocence!

Kellogg's cereal put up a huge billboard of me, calling me "The Typical American Girl." I suppose I was more or less typical. That was the image they gave me, the girl next door. I was very, very unsophisticated. I tried to be as natural as possible. My directors thought I took direction well.

Paul Leni directed me in *The Cat and the Canary*. He was very serious. He wanted me to be very coy and kittenish. I tried to do what he wanted me to do but I ended up looking pretty silly in that one. My favorite picture was *Finders Keepers* with Johnny Herron. It was Jack Oakie's film debut, and Andy Devine was in it too. It had a lot of cute scenes; it was right up my alley.

Edward Everett Horton was one of my favorites. I worked with him in *Poker Faces* and then later on the stage. We got on famously. Eddie was always very professional and very kind. He could be extremely sarcastic, of course, if he thought anybody was taking advantage of him. He was a unique personality.

When the talkies came in I said, "They won't last." I had no trouble when sound came in. I had had some experience in the theatre by then, in England. I wasn't pursuing a career in the theatre; I was there and they asked me to do it — they needed an American girl.

I retired from films after I had two children in England. I didn't care if I ever worked again. I still get fan mail — it has never stopped. I'm not buried in it, but there are a dozen or so people who have been writing me regularly for over 50 years.

Dorothy Revier

*A cameraman once told Dorothy Revier she had a face that could be pho-
tographed from any angle. A one-time Wampus Baby Star, the young
actress was a favorite of both directors and cameramen in the silent era
when she was known as "One-Take Revier."*

*Doris Velegra was born in San Francisco April 18, 1908. The self-
educated youngster made her film debut at 13 under the direction of
Harry Revier, who later became her first husband. Before long she
landed a contract with Columbia Pictures, which had a reputation for
low-budget quickies, like the other studios on Poverty Row.*

*Columbia's savior was a young gag-writer named Frank Capra,
who directed several pictures for them sans credit, circa 1926; his fre-
quent star was Revier, who earned herself the nickname of "The Queen of
Poverty Row." She got along far better with Capra than with studio boss
Harry Cohn, with whom she was romantically involved at one point.*

*"Cohn was a devil — he was tough — but he could be very kind. We
were always fighting, so I was always being fired," said Revier, who left
the studio in 1934 over personal differences with Cohn. She got the occasional call after she retired, but was forced to turn down the one part
she really wanted — Belle Whatley in* Gone With the Wind *— due to
illness.*

*"I enjoyed making movies, but it was hard work," Revier observed
in an interview at her Hollywood home. She didn't seem to miss the hard
work, but there appeared to be a longing for the glamour and excite-
ment of that long-past era. And yet, the former silent star — who took up
painting as a hobby in later years — seemed content with the peace and
solitude of her environment.*

I came from a family of artists and musicians. My education was sadly neglected. I studied dancing from the time I was 5; I started getting jobs when I was 13. Somebody saw me dancing in the Tait Cafe in San Francisco and put me in the film, *Life's Greatest Question.*

I came down to Los Angeles looking for work after that, because I thought this was where the money was. It wasn't hard at all to find work; I got a job two weeks after I came. I got an agent and found work at Universal right away. I had a chance to get a contract with them, but my agent advised me to go with Columbia. Eventually it became one of the biggest studios in Hollywood, but when I got there it was very small.

I did about six pictures with Frank Capra — *The Fate of a Flirt, Steppin' Out, When the Wife's Away* — those were all Capra pictures, even though his name wasn't on them. They were adorable little pictures. I loved working with Capra. He was very helpful; he encouraged a young person. He was a quiet, soft-spoken man. He never raised his voice.

We worked at a fairly leisurely pace in those days. There was a scene in *Submarine* where the star, Jack Holt, wanted to cry. Capra told him to go ahead and cry. And we had to sit around for an hour waiting for Jack; he was trying to cry real tears. Capra told him, "We'll take one with tears and one without — and we'll use the one that comes out best."

Actors could be very touchy in those days. I was doing a picture with Ben Lyon, and one day it came time to do his close-up and he wasn't on the set. The assistant director was furious. They got him on the set; he'd only been gone five minutes. The assistant said, "You actors, you're all alike. Horses and actors are the same." Ben said, "That's what you think, get a horse in here." And he walked off the set and didn't come back that day.

I was always treated beautifully. I worked in a lot of cheap little pictures at Columbia, but they had good actors. I never had script approval or anything like that. But one of the advantages of being under contract was that we got paid every week, whether we worked or not.

I never did two pictures at the same time, but I did one after another. There would be maybe three days rest and we'd start the next picture. There would be three productions going at once on different sets, and everybody going crazy. When I look back, it was like a mad house. But I studied hard; I pounded my lines. I never got caught short.

The acting style in silent films was very exaggerated and ridiculous. There was all that heaving and sighing and that kind of thing, but you had to do it. I liked the sound pictures much better in that way; the acting was more natural. But the atmosphere in silents was gayer, it wasn't as tense.

You weren't as nervous acting in silent films. It was easier. You didn't have to memorize lines, you just got the gist of it. You had a script with dialogue in it, and you learned it, but it was different from sound. When sound came in, the king of the realm was the sound mixer. If the sound man disliked you, he could make you sound terrible. The studio wanted to give me voice lessons, but I refused; they wanted me to speak with a phony accent.

I don't think I did too well in films. I could have gone a lot further had I had the proper handling. Dancing was my forte; I danced in only two pictures. I should never have gone into pictures. I should have stayed with my dancing, but I couldn't go to New York. I was too young; my people wouldn't allow me to go.

Mary MacLaren

From chorus girl to teenage silent film star to bit player and dress extra, Mary MacLaren had many ups and downs in the course of her career. Few movie synopses would in fact make as interesting reading as the story of her own life.

The sister of actress Katherine MacDonald, Mary MacLaren was born in Pittsburgh on January 19, 1900. Like her friend Dorothy Revier, she began her career at the tender age of 13, in a Broadway chorus line. Two years later, she made her film debut when maverick actress-producer Lois Weber spotted her in a Los Angeles stage show. Seasoned observers labeled the teenaged newcomer "a real find."

Following the blockbuster success of MacLaren's first starring vehicle, Shoes, Tod Browning took her under his directorial wing and guided her through a series of pictures. Her most memorable role came in 1921, when she played Queen Anne of Austria opposite Douglas Fairbanks Sr. as D'Artagnan in first film version of The Three Musketeers.

MacLaren had been demoted to supporting roles by the time she quit Hollywood in 1924 to marry a Scottish colonel in the Indian army. She later returned to the screen playing small parts, often without billing; a bit in the Marx Brothers' madcap A Day at the Races was but one among two decades of unheralded roles. Injuries sustained in a serious auto accident forced her to retire.

In 1952 MacLaren wrote a novel called The Twisted Heart, about a young woman who discovered her husband was a homosexual. The story was rather daring in its day; late in life the author observed, "I think now my book and time have caught up with each other."

MacLaren was interviewed in her Hollywood home, purchased in 1917 with earnings from her movies. Despite her advancing years, she was cheerful and upbeat. But the one-time silent star, an animal lover *who befriended homeless cats and dogs, fell on hard times in her last years.*

In 1979 county officials tried to declare MacLaren incompetent, claiming she was living in "submarginal conditions" — which, sadly, was not far from the truth. But she won court battles against both county bureaucrats and a self-styled "bishop" who tried to claim possession of her property, and the community rallied around her.

My mother had studied to go on the stage; she gave up any thought of it when she met my father. In 1911, when I was 11 years old, we moved to New York. My sister immediately went to work at the Wintergarden as an understudy. When I was 13 I said, "Mother, I want to go on the stage," and I went into the chorus at the Wintergarden.

I was in *The Passing Show of 1914* and then *Dancin' Around* with Al Jolson. They were going to go on tour. I said, "The show is going to California, mother; let's go with it." She said, "We can't go, we have our furniture..." I said, "Let's break it up, burn it up or give it away, but let's go."

My mother got a job in the wardrobe department and we went on tour, playing all these big cities. It was wonderful; I was only 15. We played the Morosco Theatre in Los Angeles, and then we went to San Francisco. Diamond Jim Brady threw a great big party there, but my mother wouldn't let me go — something I've always regretted.

We returned to L.A. and I decided I had to get some work. I went back to the Morosco and did *So Long Lettie* with Charlotte Greenwood, and another show. Lois Weber came to see the show, and she set up an appointment for me at Universal. I was thrilled.

The first day on the lot, Lois showed me a copy of *Collier's* magazine; it had this heart-rending story in it called *Shoes*. And she said, "Mary, I took a second look at you, and decided you would be it." Right away the studio put me in *Where Are My*

Children? with Tyrone Power Sr., just to get me acquainted with being in front of a camera.

Shoes made $3 million for Universal. The story is that this young girl is working in a 5-and-10-cent store, and her shoes are hopelessly worn out. Her father is an alcoholic. This poor girl ends up selling herself for a new pair of shoes.

After I did this film I had an appointment with Cecil B. De Mille at Paramount. I had gone to the park and plucked this beautiful rose for him. He was very pleased with the rose, but he was a bit too forward with me, as a young girl. This woman came into the office while we were talking and she said, "Cecil, will I be seeing you tomorrow morning?" And he said, "Yes. Where shall I see you, here or in bed?' That was the most shocking thing I had ever heard in my life.

Valentino's dressing room was next to mine at Universal. I loved him; he was such a gentle man. He'd come into my dressing room and take me in his arms and give me a big hug and a kiss, and he'd say, "I have to start the day out right." I loved Douglas Fairbanks too, because he was so full of vitality. He had no inhibitions about him. He said, "I'm a show off, I admit it — so what?" It just endeared him to me.

I starred in six or seven pictures, but I worked in so many films later on; I did a lot of bit parts. I was on a picture at MGM with Jeanette MacDonald and Nelson Eddy. The director, W.S. Van Dyke, came up to me; he said, "How are things going?" I said, "Not too ill and not too well." He put me in every picture of his after that. One day they were ready to go to work; he looked around and said, "Where's Mary?" The assistant said, "I guess she's at home." Van Dyke said, "Work will start when she gets here."

Mary MacLaren died of respiratory problems in a Hollywood hospital on November 9, 1985. She was 85 years old.

Eleanor Boardman

Unlike Mary MacLaren, Eleanor Boardman had no intention of becoming an actress. She fell into it by chance and quickly became a star, though her career was short-lived by choice. She also became the real-life leading lady of two of Hollywood's more individualistic directors.

Born in Philadelphia on August 19, 1898, Eleanor Boardman originally planned a career as an artist. Fate decreed otherwise. She made her film debut in Souls for Sale *in 1923, and followed it with* Vanity Fair. *She was a young starlet when she gained fame by posing for an advertisement as "The Eastman Kodak Girl."*

Director King Vidor fell in love with the face in the ad and starred Boardman in his modestly-budgeted Three Wise Fools, *the first of five pictures they would make together. They were married in 1925 after he was divorced from his first wife, actress Florence Arto Vidor, and had two daughters; they themselves divorced in 1933.*

Although Boardman is remembered chiefly today for Vidor's 1928 masterpiece, The Crowd *— a stark drama that focused on "the average man" and depicted the dark side of the American dream — she appeared in a number of pictures. Among others, she was featured with Lon Chaney Sr. in* Tell It to the Marines; *the prehistoric two-color Technicolor* Mamba; *and Cecil B. De Mille's 1931 remake of his early silent epic,* The Squaw Man.

In the '50s, the former model served as the Paris fashion correspondent for Harper's Bazaar. *Long retired, she is the widow of film director Henri D'Abbabie D'Arrast (Topaze) and lives near Santa Barbara, California.*

I went to New York to attend the Academy of Fine Arts. I took some of my costume sketches to Goldwyn Studios, and they said, "Would you rather have a screen test?" I said no. But they said they wanted to arrange one, so I said okay. After they did the test they said, "You leave Tuesday for the Coast."

I didn't know anybody out in Los Angeles. I had never done any acting, taken any lessons or anything before I came out. But I photographed well, that was the thing. They were interested in new faces, so they signed me to a seven- year contract; I made two pictures and they extended it to seven more years.

Louis B. Mayer was a real son of a bitch. There was one film I refused to do. He said if I didn't do it, he'd put me in a bad film with a bad director, and he'd ruin me. He said I *had* to do it. I told King Vidor, and he said, "Do you think for one moment that Mayer is going to spend money on a bad film?"

The Crowd was to be the first picture without glamour — that was Vidor's intent when he made it. In every picture up to that time, people had lived happily ever after. *The Big Parade* had been a big success; it had pulled MGM out of debt, and they asked Vidor what he wanted to do next. Irving Thalberg told him he could do anything he wanted. He said, "I'll take John and Mary Doe — no education, no money, two children, living over the El in New York..." MGM was afraid of the film because it had no glamour; it was downbeat. It did better in Europe than it did here.

The early silents were very broad in getting things across, and that was what Vidor wanted to get away from. As they say, he wanted to tell it like it is. *The Crowd* told its story with the camera; it was unique in that way. It was the first realistic portrayal of life on the screen.

Even *The Big Parade* was natural in its acting, though. In fact, they originally filmed John Gilbert coming home from the war on both legs. Vidor said he should come home with one — he went out on a Sunday and took a shot of Gilbert walking back

With James Murray in King Vidor's masterpiece, *The Crowd* (1928).

home with one leg. He showed it to Thalberg, and he agreed — it had greater impact with one leg.

My directors often let me do the scene the way I wanted. They didn't know I didn't know anything. But Vidor changed very little of what I did. He let you do it your way, then he would talk it over with you if he wanted to change something.

It was very easy working on a film with Vidor; the cast was always like a family. He was very gentle as a director, not too authoritative. There was no screaming, like with Cecil B. De Mille. I saw De Mille give some of his ammunition to other people, though he never did to me.

I don't regret being in films instead of pursuing a career in art. It was a more glamorous life. It was fun being in pictures, but it was work. My one regret was that I didn't get to do *A Farewell to Arms* with Gary Cooper. Paramount promised it to me, then the studio stuck me in something else and I didn't get to do it.

I went to Europe soon afterwards. I liked it there and I lived in different countries for about 12 years. I put Hollywood and that lifestyle behind me; I wasn't interested in making films any more. Europe was much more interesting.

BRING ON THE CLOWNS

Marcel Marceau

Marcel Marceau has won universal acclaim as the greatest living prac-
titioner of pantomime, an art form which can be traced back over 2,000
years. Since his first U.S. tour in 1955, countless young performers have
learned to speak "the language of silence."

The younger son of a butcher, Marcel Mangel was born in Stras-
bourg, France, March 22, 1923. As a child he sat entranced in movie
theatres watching Charlie Chaplin, his idol from the age of 5; he began
imitating birds and play- acting with other children, dreaming of a career
in the theatre. At the outbreak of World War II he fled German-occupied
Strasbourg for southwestern France. At 17, he joined the Resistance
with his older brother, Alain, who would later become his personal repre-
sentative.

In 1945 Marceau enrolled in the School of Dramatic Art, where he
studied acting with Charles Dullin and mime with Étienne Decroux. He
served a stint in the First French Army before joining Jean-Louis Bar-
rault in his company at the Théâtre de Marigny, where he won acclaim
as Arlequin in Baptiste. *He then created his alter ego, Bip, and toured*
western Europe.

After his mimodrama Death Before Dawn *won the Deburau Prize*
(named for the great nineteenth-century mime), he formed Compagnie de
Mime Marcel Marceau in 1949. The following year he met childhood
idol Stan Laurel, who befriended the little-known artist and helped to
promote him.

With his own company, Marceau presented a series of full-scale
mimodramas, beginning with an adaptation of Gogol's The Overcoat
(1951) which later toured the United States. While he has created many
other sophisticated mimodramas — including Candide, *which he di-*
rected and starred in for the Ballet Company of the Hamburg Opera —

short style mimes as elementary as Walking Against the Wind *have made him famous throughout the world.*

Although he was "known among theatregoers," Marceau did not achieve wide renown until he began performing on television. He won an Emmy for his first appearance on American TV, with Maurice Chevalier, returning for a series of specials with Red Skelton "that opened up a mass audience I otherwise would never have reached." He has appeared in a number of short films, several of which have won awards; among his feature appearances are Barbarella *and Mel Brooks'* Silent Movie, *in which he spoke the singular line of dialogue.*

When Marceau talks there is an almost wild fascination in his eyes; his thoughts move through a strange and convoluted process, hands jumping to describe a snake's slither or a butterfly's flutter, his imagination running at full gallop. He speaks not so much words as ideas, projecting them with the much same energy and speed he exhibits on stage.

I was the first to recreate the mime theatre, which didn't exist any more. The art of mime was lost; we remembered it only because we had silent film actors like Chaplin, Keaton, Laurel and Hardy. Étienne Decroux created a new grammar, a language of mime. I learned his grammar, and then when I created my character Bip I added a style to it, a new dimension of technique.

There were only a few studying mime until I became popular, then Decroux had students coming from all over the world. I am grateful that he was my teacher. Maybe we didn't get along, but I was not bad propaganda for him; I didn't carry the bad word.

I could be very rich, because very few artists have toured so much as I have — but for 15 years, all the money that I had went to support my company. The money I had was always serving an artistic purpose. The more you have money, the less freedom you have: an unfortunate parallel. If Chaplin had performed with his own company, he would not have had the freedom he had.

As his alter ego, Bip, "brother" to Chaplin's Little Tramp.

Offstage, a vibrant conversationalist.

In the dual role of a deaf-mute puppeteer and his elderly benefactor, in the William Castle film, *Shanks* (1974).

Bip is akin to Chaplin, Keaton... we deal with the same emotions — love, frustration — we make people laugh and cry for the same reasons, touching the heart through love and through compassion. We are the eternal fools and clowns that are a part of every man, which is why he identifies with the clown — because life is just a big theatre.

An artist has to live a total life, and this is why an artist is not only an entertainer. I like the public to laugh and to cry, but I like also... to create consciousness in their minds. I am a silent witness of my time — I speak out without words.

I don't like it to be said that I want to get a message to man. There is an inside force which pushes me to recreate the dreams of man, to put this into gestures — and then I become a philosopher without wanting to be one. I become a moralist without wanting to be one. And I remain a clown, wanting to be a clown.

A mime artist has not really to tell a story, he has to create magic and style within the frame of a work. The numbers that are remembered are the ones that retain the style and the meaning also — *The Mask Maker, The Creation of the World, Bip in the Modern and Future Life* — each one has its qualities. You create a number and it goes for years, but you have to keep pace with your number, because like children — not every child is beautiful, but every child has a quality which can make it beautiful if he works hard on it.

The older you get, the better you have to become. If you don't grow, you just quit. Unfortunately a man has not seven lives. But he can project his art through film, through books, through schools — what man creates and gives in his time is not lost; it is recreated so that man has an everlasting life. Men die, but other men take up their ideas.

My work has become deeper over the years, I think... numbers like *The Creation of the World* and *The Hands* are more spiritual and more with the philosophy of life, the quality of style. Bip has grown also, he has matured — at the beginning he was only a skater. Now he is concerned with the future, or dreams he is Don Juan. He has matured in style, but he still has the sincerity of a man who struggles with windmills, like Don Quixote.

Bip in the Modern and Future Life shows that we know about pushing buttons, elevators, mechanical stairs; we know about the adaptation of man to a system which is mechanical. But the day the system fails, man is helpless. I show him entering the world of the future, which is going back to his subconscious, back to the womb of his mother and recreating life — all his dreams and frustrations — and going back to the cycle of man, to the ape, finding two stones and creating light through fire.

There is recreated a new son of man who is torn between metal and flesh, between the will of remaining a Romantic man and maybe a need to progress — creating mechanization and trying to escape from it, finding more purity in himself and going back to nature; trying to be one's self and not trapped in a preprogrammed society.

Many people compare *Modern and Future Life* to *2001: A Space Odyssey*. I created it at the same time, but I had not seen the film. I am a great admirer of Ray Bradbury; I think much of his work could be adapted to mimodramas. I love science fiction, I love the *fantastique* and the supernatural — we need the Gods on stage. We need the inspiration of the supernatural; we need this power, this magic in the theatre.

Pantomime deals with the supernatural, in a certain sense. To recreate the world on a stage... to show the elements appear and disappear, a snake becoming an apple and an apple becoming a love and a love becoming a sin, and the warning of God chasing Adam and Eve through paradise — all these symbolic gestures are in a way supernatural.

Also the timing aspect is supernatural. Real timing has its course but in the theatre there is a sense of timing which is elliptic, the condensation of time — to play life from birth to death in three minutes [*Youth, Maturity, Old Age and Death*] is of course supernatural. When you say "supernatural," it's creating magic on the stage but it's also making life bigger as you can conceive it on a stage.

When you show for the public an experience, it should be something very well conceived. The public may be lost by something, but it should at least disturb them; it should be done with style and perfection. This is what an artist has to care about: style, perfection and touching the public.

But in no way an artist has to want only to please the public, because very often life is bigger than reality. What is real to us can suddenly be overthrown by something we don't expect — and that is where the supernatural arrives in life.

An artist has to experience in his traumatism, in his world, in his subconscious; he has to fix on the stage the world we live in. Not only the world, but all the ideas he gets from imagining a world. All what he senses the public does not sense; like a seeing brother he has to show them the light. An artist should be ahead of his time, even when they are witnesses and they reflect their time.

Red Skelton

There is a satisfaction in performing for live audiences that Red Skelton thrives on, like his friend Marcel Marceau. When his long-running television show was unceremoniously dumped from the air in 1971, Skelton dropped out of the Hollywood rat race and turned his back on the medium that made him a household name; today, he still plays Las Vegas, but prefers the college circuit, along with conventions and state fairs.

Richard Skelton was born July 18, 1913, in Vincennes, Indiana. He grew up in poverty, the youngest of four boys. The youngster was selling newspapers on a Vincennes street corner for a penny apiece when comedian Ed Wynn bought a paper and gave him a ticket for his evening performance. Skelton liked the show so much he decided to become a comic himself.

At 12, he ran away from home to join a medicine show; he performed in riverboat minstrel shows, circuses, carnivals, burlesque shows and Walkathons (Depression era dance marathons) before he found stardom on the vaudeville circuit.

In 1938 Skelton made his feature film debut in RKO's Having Wonderful Time. *After supplying "comic relief" in MGM's* Flight Command, *a series of star vehicles followed, including* Whistling in Brooklyn, A Southern Yankee *(his favorite),* The Fuller Brush Man *and* The Clown, *a remake of* The Champ.

Skelton continued to do his popular CBS radio program when he made his television debut with a "live" show on NBC in 1951, distrusting the new medium. His weekly Red Skelton Show *ran 17 seasons on CBS TV (1953-70), switching to NBC for the final year. Freddie the Freeloader, Clem Kadiddlehopper, George Appleby and San Fernando Red were among the characterizations he brought to his audiences.*

The comedian was interviewed when he surfaced in Anaheim, California, for a personal appearance, in a rare excursion from the

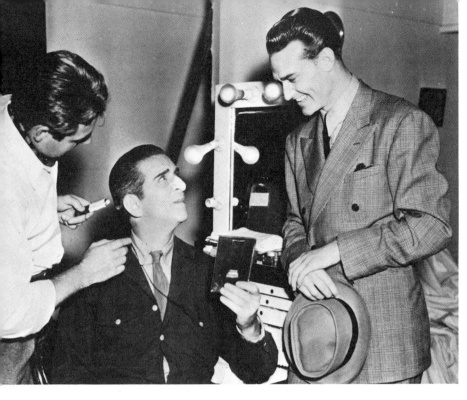

The young vaudeville comic, visiting veteran actor Edward Everett Horton on an RKO soundstage, 1937.

With young Zero Mostel, in *Dubarry Was a Lady* (1943).

Red in grey, with Minor Watson (holding map) in his favorite film, *A Southern Yankee* (1948).

As Freddie the Freeloader, with Robert Vaughn on *The Red Skelton Show.*

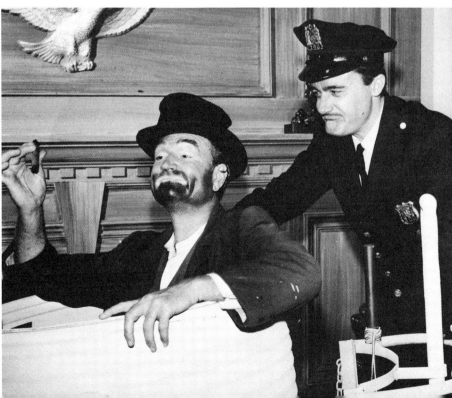

nation's hinterlands. While noticeably bitter about the industry's cavalier dismissal of him as "passé," Skelton seemed content. "I don't take life seriously because you're not going to get out of it alive," he quipped.

While his longtime dream of a performing arts school has never materialized, there is scarcely a dull moment in the life of the aging court jester, and never an idle one: "I thump out five musical selections on the piano every morning. Then I write out an idea for a short story — at the end of the week I take the best one and complete it. After a performance at night, I take out my paints and do an outline. I also do needlepoint. In my spare time, I fix my bicycle. I sleep about two and a half hours a night."

In recent years, Skelton has garnered a flock of honors. In 1986 he was given a honorary doctor of humanities degree from Ball State University in Muncie, Indiana, and the prestigious Governor's Award from the Academy of Television Arts and Sciences. The following year, the Screen Actors Guild presented him with their Annual Achievement Award for his achievements as a performer and an humanitarian.

My father died two months before I was born. When I was about 8, I told my mother I wanted to be an entertainer. Then she told me my father had traveled with the Hagenbeck & Wallace circus. She said, "I knew it would come out in one of you boys; I didn't know which one."

I'll never forget when I was a boy, my grandmother was dying. We were all standing around her bedside talking, whispering. She said, "Talk louder. I know I'm dying, but I may still learn something." That has stayed with me all through the years.

I like going out and meeting people, finding out things. I talk to people on the street. I'll go shopping; people will come up to me and they'll tell me what they like, what they dislike. Before I went on TV I used to go to parties; I accepted invitations. And I'd get up and perform because I wanted to see what they would laugh at in their living room that they wouldn't laugh at in the theatre.

You can't lie to the camera. It tells the truth. I like people — I have no hatred towards any people — and I think it comes across. People come up to me and ask, "Why are you nice to everybody you meet?" I was told that man was made in God's image. I've never met God, and the next guy just might be him — and I don't mean George Burns, either.

People who can't find God aren't looking for him — same reason a robber can't find a policeman. There was a woman who said she didn't believe in God, and she knew she was going to die soon. I asked if she was going to be buried. She said yes. I asked how it felt to be all dressed up and have no place to go.

Theatre is *my* temple. When they book me they ask, "Can you do 40 minutes?" I say, "Hell, I bow for that long." They take me over to the auditorium, push me out there, and then figure out a way to get me off. When I play colleges I tell the young people, "You may not remember me, but I'm the guy that made it possible for you to stay up late."

CBS said I was through — that I didn't mean anything, that my comedy was passé. They said they were going to come in with more modern things. When I make personal appearances I generally get three to five standing ovations.

Television is one of the greatest things that's come along since the rubber end on the pencil. But it's being misused. It's not for the public. The networks don't care about the public; they throw anything at 'em and people accept it. If they can sell fear on television — subliminally — and people are afraid to go out, they stay home. So they watch TV. If they watch TV the networks sell more commercial time.

I created several of my characters on radio. People ask how Junior, the Mean Widdle Kid, came about: I was trying to live a childhood I never had. People thought some of my characters really existed. I'll still get $5 in an envelope at Christmas time for Freddie the Freeloader.

An expectant father's "moment of truth," in a TV pantomime sketch.

The Old Man Watching the Parade was something I did for my little boy, Richard. He had brought home a record of "The Bridge on the River Kwai." I was just clowning around and trying to make him laugh. He liked it and called in his mother. Then I started working on it. I went down to the studio and called everybody together; I did it for them, and they all sat there and they were crying.

A lot of people think that clowns are sad. That's because when you're seeing them perform, you're seeing them at their best. When clowns are offstage, though — if you walked around like that all the time, they'd throw a net over you. I've escaped many a time.

Young people who want to do comedy will start out doing what they think is good. And they're accepted. But then they become victims of laughter. It's a dangerous thing for any comedian. They'll do something off-color, and it'll get a big laugh. So they'll throw in another one. Next thing you know, what they started out to do they've pushed aside, and they're doing what everybody else does — sex jokes. They don't need off-color jokes. It gets a laugh at the time, but the audience doesn't remember it when they walk out; they use it against you.

Young performers must develop their own technique, their own delivery. You can't take other people's stuff. They say imitation is the highest form of flattery — I think it's the lowest form of thievery.

I'm not really a master of my craft; I'm still learning. My comedy is more sincere today. You look more for the dignity than for the laugh. You take little short cuts. It's down to where you've made a study of something; it becomes so natural it looks like it's just on the spur of the moment — like when I sneeze and my shoes fly off. I always work that way; I don't plan anything.

When I say, "Good night, and may God bless" at the end of my show — that's *me* talking. When I thank people for coming I think they know deep down in their heart that I'm saying, "You are my family." The audience is the only family that I've ever had; since I was 10 years old, that's the only thing I've known.

147

Doodles Weaver

Doodles Weaver was a "wild and crazy guy" long before the current crop of comedians were born. He was best known for the nutty comedy routines and songs like "The William Tell Overture" ("...and there goes the winner — Fee-tle-baum") he performed on records, road tours, radio and TV with Spike Jones and his City Slickers.

Winstead Sheffield Weaver was born May 11, 1911, the scion of a prominent Los Angeles family. He was graduated Phi Beta Kappa from Stanford University, where he garnered a reputation as a prankster, to become a popular nightclub comic. He made his first assault on the Broadway stage in Meet the People *(1940) and later returned for* Marinka.

When his five-year association with Spike Jones ended due to a personality clash in 1951, he starred in The Doodles Weaver Show *on NBC; he later did a Saturday morning kiddie program and a syndicated series of sketches entitled* A Day With Doodles. *In the '70s, he played the recurring role of Eddie Hoyle on* Starsky and Hutch, *and recorded the album* Feetlebaum Returns.

Weaver appeared in over 100 films and TV movies during his career, following his feature debut in Come and Get It. *His favorite picture was Cecil B. De Mille's* The Story of Dr. Wassell; The Ladies Man, *one of several with Jerry Lewis, was another.*

It was a morose and melancholy man who granted an interview a few months before his death. "Don't expect me to entertain you," he warned at the outset. "All my life I've been funny and clever but I can't do it any more. I can't make people laugh because I feel lousy."

Before long, however, Doodles was singing, playing the piano, doing charades and making funny faces and cracking jokes. "Thirty-eight-foot sailboat," he announced, grabbing a plastic model from the bookshelf — then turned it over to reveal 38 little plastic feet glued to the bottom. There was a lot of pain in that final performance — but a great deal of courage, too.

When I was little my mother would play the piano and I'd sing, "Yankee Doodle Went to London..." That was how I got my name; the kids called me "Yankee Doodle." I come from a refined aristocratic family — but who's going to call a kid Winstead?

There was always one or two guys in school who were the class clown. I was the comic, but I was also captain of the basketball team; I played football too. I didn't go into show business to beat out Jack Benny or be another Chaplin. I went into it because it was right here in Los Angeles, and I was eccentric and tall and I knew lots of people in the business — that was the only way to get in. It was fun, it easy to do, and it paid well.

I started around 1932. Being from L.A. I got to know the different guys whose fathers went to Stanford or USC — these people were all in show business. There were a few nightclubs in L.A. like the Trocadero but nobody used comedians in those days; you had to go to New York to be a comic.

After all these years I spent developing a character and a personality, the first part I played in Hollywood was a goofy Western rodeo hick who tried to saddle a horse. Then I went out to Hal Roach Studios to be introduced, and I walked out with a $250 a week contract. My father was disgusted. He spent a lot of money to send me to Stanford, to be something, and here I am making $250 a week, doing nothing but driving a Cadillac, smoking cigars and drinking whiskey with John Barrymore.

During the war I was with Horace Heidt. I went into special services — at times I did 14 shows in one day, at hospitals. When the war was over I became a professional nightclub entertainer. Jobs were everywhere, there were lots of clubs. Guys were coming back from overseas; the clubs were always packed. It was like Las Vegas without gambling.

The hotels had shows, the clubs had shows; they all used guys like me. I was working in a nightclub called the Bandbox — Phil Foster worked there, Buddy Hackett, Milton Berle. You'd

Doodles on woodwinds, far right, with Freddie Morgan, Dick Morgan (banjo), Dr. Horatio Q. Birdbath, Helen Grayco, George Rock (trumpet) and Spike Jones in *The Musical Depreciation Revue.*

play about a month, then you'd make the rounds of clubs. It was a good life.

The guys you see on TV — David Letterman, Jonathan Winters, Dom de Luise, Richard Pryor — they're not a bit funny, not to me. If I did stuff like Pryor does they'd take me and put me in jail. My competition were guys who worked to be funny. We had a different audience every night — we didn't have signs that said, "Applause." Phil Foster would walk out and say, "How do you like me so far?" That's funny. I'd come out and say, "You know how to milk a mouse? First, you get a small stool…"

I could do imitations, but I was versatile — Rich Little is good, but ask him to sit down and play Chopin. I'd sing a song, do a pantomime. I hadn't even heard of Red Skelton; I was doing the "Guzzler's Gin" sketch three years before him — I got it from Fred Allen, who was doing it way back. I called it "Dribbler's Gin."

I didn't join Spike Jones until 1946. He had signed to do a tour, and he was enlarging his show. He had asked me to join him before, but I didn't like vaudeville, doing four or five shows a day; I didn't want to go with him because it was too much work. There's no sense doing four shows a day when you can do one.

Spike said, "We're going to do a month's tour with the City Slickers. We've got a girl singer who does funny stuff, and a juggler, and your act would fit right in; you can also play the clarinet or do whatever you want. Plus I'll get you two weeks in a movie, *Variety Girl*." I played a trumpet player who dives off the end of the diving board. I dove underwater; when the bubbles came up the notes would come out.

The movie turned out fine and I got along with him well. I went on tour with him and we played to packed houses. My nightclub acts all fit in; I did "Chloe" and I helped write some other things for him, which was not hard to do, because I'd been doing that kind of stuff myself — "I Surrender, Dear" — I'd act out the words. It was similar to what Spike was doing, where you made noises acting out the songs. Musical charades was all it was.

I was doing the horse race ["William Tell"] and other routines before I joined Spike; I started doing it in nightclubs before the war. I made up the character of Professor Feetlebaum when I was working in the clubs. It was from the race — "and Fee-tle-baum." It was entirely accidental. I used to have a different ending for the race, when I was doing it in 1939, '40, at the clubs.

I'd use a funny word and everybody would laugh — "...and there goes the winner — Glibwicket. There goes the winner — Pootwaddle. There goes the winner — Gackengoofer." When I said "Feetlebaum" one time, everybody laughed about twice as much.

I wore a funny wig, a bald head with blonde hair sticking out of the sides, something like Ed Wynn would do. I'd reach in my pocket and pull this thing on and say, "And here's Professor Feetlebaum." I'd hit my nose on the microphone and then start to do a song and get all mixed up with the words.

There was a guy named Roy Atwell who used to do a news item. He'd say, "Good evening, fiends, I mean friends." Spoonerism is an old form of humor. I took spoonerisms out of talking and put them into music. I used to get more laughs in ten minutes than Steve Martin gets in an hour.

Spike was very serious with his work, and he looked serious all the time, but that was part of his act, being a deadpan. If you were doing something funny, it was all right; if you were doing something serious, then he didn't like funny stuff.

Spike's *Musical Depreciation Revue* changed very little from the time I started until the end, almost no change at all. It was as great as any five years I ever had. We had a lot of fun, we made a lot of money, there was no war, no troubles, no gripes; we went to the best restaurants. The people treated us like kings. They'd meet us at the train and take us around in their cars; they'd be looking forward for two or three months each time to our visit. The people couldn't do enough for us.

The sad joke is, we all have to quit. I don't want to quit, but I don't feel good. I've tried everything. I've been to the doctors; I had the heart by-pass; it didn't make any difference. I've tried all the different magic pills. Nothing is funny when you don't feel good.

Doodles Weaver died of self-inflicted gunshot wounds on January 13, 1983, at his home in Burbank, California; he was 71 years old.

Mousie Garner

"I'd like to play "Tea for Two" from the picture Ben Hur," *the pianist would announce. The unrecognizable tune that followed soon dissolved into chaos, as the maestro banged the keyboard with his elbows, his hip, his nose and occasionally his hands. At the finish, he went into convulsions, slapped himself, fell off the piano bench and fell flat on his face.*

Mousie Garner was a fixture at the Mayfair Music Hall in Santa Monica, California, in the '70s and early '80s. During the show's intermission, he would mercilessly pummel the piano in the lobby, spewing out song fragments and impressions of people like Jimmy Durante and Fats Waller ("Honeysuckle Rose" withered under his touch).

Paul A. Garner was born in Washington, D.C., in 1909. He aspired to be cartoonist, then planned a career in classical music until he broke his left hand. While still in his teens he toured with an act called Jack Pepper with Mustard and Ketchup (he was Mustard). He served a short stint as a replacement for one of the Three Stooges when the original trio left their mentor, Ted Healy, in the early '30s; he and his partners toured as the Gentlemaniacs when the original comics rejoined Healy.

In 1954 Spike Jones hired him to replace Doodles Weaver's frizzy-haired colleague, Sir Fredric Gas. After six years on the road with Jones, wreaking havoc with songs like "You Always Hurt the One You Love" and Weaver's old chestnut, "Chloe," he busied himself with television assignments.

Garner, who had a recurring role as a waiter on Surfside 6, *has been featured on a variety of other programs. Among his recent film appearances are* Cheech and Chong's Next Movie *and the TV movie,* The Dream Merchants.

I was stagestruck pretty early; I started [as a musician] when I was a young boy. Finally I got a job at the Earl Theatre in Washington, D.C., with my cousin, Jack Wolf. They were called presentation theatres. They had live stage shows with the orchestra in the pit and the band on stage; I played with the band. The talkies came in and the theatre went sound, so that was the end of that.

Jack Pepper, the emcee, got a job in Baltimore, so he took Wolf and me to work with him in his act. We went with him thinking we would only be there one or two weeks, because we were under age. He talked my mother and father into letting me go on the road. That was in 1928; I've been on the road ever since.

Wolf and I were just doing straight songs at first. A guy on the bill with us said, "I think I can make you guys funny, but don't tell Pepper." We went to a pawnshop and bought a couple of suits — my partner bought a tail suit so tight on him he couldn't breathe. My suit was just the opposite — three times too big. We brought out the piano and we got a laugh right away. Pepper started singing; he was so nervous, he took his ukelele and broke it across my head.

In 1931 we heard that Ted Healy wanted to replace the Three Stooges. Moe, Shemp and Larry left Ted and went out on the road; they weren't allowed to use the name Stooges because Healy owned the name. Jack Wolf and a fellow named Dick Hakins and I went down to the Imperial Theatre where Healy was holding auditions. There must've been 100 guys there.

What do you think my audition was? Healy gave me a bang in the head. He smacked me in the head and I jumped on him and bit his ear and grabbed his nose. He said, "Get in the corner. You're hired."

It was all improvisation with Healy; I didn't know what the hell I was doing. A whack in the head, a poke in the eyes... he knocked me on my ass once; I bit him on the leg. Healy would say, "What time is it?" I'd say, "One o'clock." He'd give me a bong in the head. I'd say, "I'm glad it ain't 12." The jokes weren't funny; the whack in the head protected the jokes.

Hakins, Wolf and I went into a show called *The Gang's All Here*, a big Broadway show with Ruby Keeler. Then Healy got another show, *Crazy Quilt* with Fanny Brice. That ran almost two years; then we got an offer, so we left Ted and went into vaude-ville. Moe, Larry and Shemp came back, then Curly replaced Shemp and they went into pictures.

We couldn't use the name Stooges, so we called ourselves The Gentlemaniacs. What Moe, Larry and Curly did with the smack-ing, the poking in the eyes, we did with instruments — breaking fiddles across heads, squirting seltzer bottles. In 1936 Hakins and I and a guy named Sammy Wolfe rejoined Healy. He tried to make another Three Stooges out of us but it was too late; the other three guys had made it.

These comics today are marvelous; I enjoy 'em. But they get up there and all they do is talk. Talk and talk and talk. I like to give 'em some music, give 'em a little entertainment. I can stand up and tell jokes, but I don't think it's going to pay off for me. I be-lieve in what I'm doing, and I think my style of comedy is going to come around again. I believe in homespun fun — slapstick with good taste.

The kids are my audience today. They're the best audience. They say, "That's new." I have to tell them, "No, it's what I used to do. But I put an '80s twist on it." My attitude of working is differ-ent today. I used to work three times as fast; now I slow down, I take my time.

Clyde Cook

"I used to do peculiar things — headspins, shoulder rolls, flip-flap som-
ersaults, round-off twisters — things people had never seen. I did stuff
like this, too," said the diminutive Australian comic, getting to his feet.
His legs straight, he bent from the waist, grabbed his ankles and looked
out between his knees.

For a man of 88, it was no mean feat. But Clyde Cook, whose eccen-
tric dancing and acrobatic clowning once earned him the nickname of
The Kangaroo Boy, made light of his agility. "I exercise," he said with a
shrug.

Cook was born December 16, 1891, in Port McQuarrie, Australia,
some 400 miles outside Sydney, where he grew up. He started as a danc-
er at the age of six; at 16 he went to London, where he worked his way up
from the variety circuit to a headline act at the prestigious Alhambra.

He played the Folies-Bergère and the Ziegfeld Follies before he came
to Hollywood in 1920, where he enjoyed a short-lived popularity in
two-reel comedies billing him as "The Funniest Man on Earth." He
spent the last two decades of his career as a highly-dependable — and
highly-priced — character actor, working for directors like Howard
Hawks (The Dawn Patrol), John Ford (Wee Willie Winkie) and
Michael Curtiz (The Sea Hawk.)

Cook was one of the last survivors of the English music hall, as it
existed at the beginning of the century, when he was interviewed at his
home near Santa Barbara, California. His outlook on life was as sunny
as the warm spring weather, his accent as thick as the proverbial
London fog.

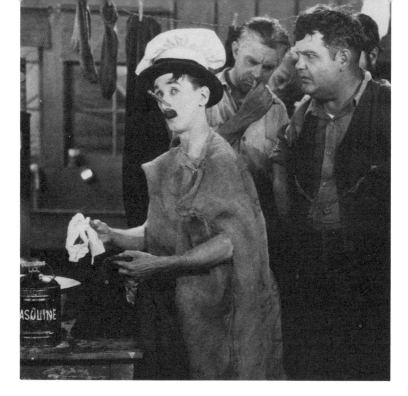

With Oliver "Babe" Hardy in *Wandering Papas* (1925), directed by Stan Laurel; clowning at his home near Santa Barbara, California, in 1980.

photo by the author

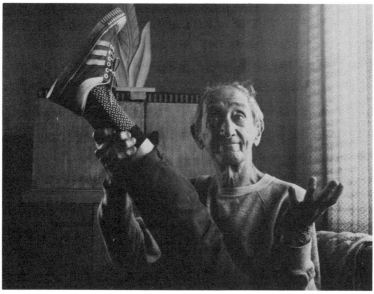

When I was 7 or 8, my mother started me on the piano. Then they started me dancing, because I could do the Highland Fling. I got very good at dancing — clog dancing, Irish jigs and all that. They used to have fights at one of the old theatres in Sydney. Before the fight, some guy who thought he could sing would get up and do one of these old English ballads, and they would throw sixpence or something into the ring. Then I'd come out and dance, do somersaults and stuff. I used to make about 12 shillings and sixpence — about $10 a night — and that went a long way in my household.

There was an outfit called Williamson's Theatre that put on pantomimes; they'd import American acts and English comedians, and all the bloody Australians would get the smaller parts. I started as an understudy when I was about 13; one year I was the ass part of a donkey in one of the pantomimes. When I was about 16 some people in the show said, "Boy, you ought to go to England, or America, that's what you ought to do." America scared the crap out of me...

I worked my passage from Australia painting out the storeroom, and went to London. I arrived in December and it was snowing. There was a little place in Trafalgar Square where performers congregated. You could get a cup of tea for a penny — anything to keep the bloody cold away. They sold baked potatoes at night, and I used to get two of them and push 'em in my pockets, to keep my hands warm.

Eventually I managed to get what they called a deputy. They had all these little variety theatres where they had Sir Harry Lauder and all these people. To make your money in it, you had to play two theatres a night, and you traveled by carriage. I went out and played one of these places — the Ilford Palace or something — and the moment I came on stage to go into my act, a guy said, "Get off, will ya?"

I went out to one of the higher class theatres in London; W.C.

Fields was one of the acts on the bill, as a juggler. Then I was signed to play all the theatres in the circuit — Manchester, Liverpool, Glasgow, Edinburgh, Wales. I was engaged to go to Germany for a month, then I went to Ireland, just before the Sinn Fein business. They'd have booked me all over the bloody world if I hadn't stopped them.

I played the Folies-Bergère and then I went with Andre Charlot, who started the London Alhambra. I stayed with him for three years and got to be quite a big shot, I suppose; I worked with Gertrude Lawrence and Beatrice Lillie.

Then the First World War broke out. I got called up; I served on a ship for a while, then returned to Australia and put on shows. I was in Melbourne when the Armistice was signed. The newspaper came out with an extra edition about 9:15 at night — I got a paper and ran out on stage and showed it to everybody. And nothing happened. I said "Peace has been signed," and went off to nothing. I think the shock was too great for them.

After the war I came to America. I was engaged on my name to play some vaudeville. I didn't like this "Two Shows a Day," so I quit. I was walking along Broadway and I bumped into an acrobat who had worked in the Folies-Bergère. He was rehearsing at the New York Hippodrome. I went with him, and I watched all these people rehearse their stuff. R.H. Burnside, the producer, came up to me. He said, "I could place you in this show." I stayed there for a year.

I'd be alone on the stage with a bucket and sponge and a piece of soap. I used to climb up and down this ladder, and then I'd go into my eccentric dancing. While I was there Winifred Sheehan from Fox Film Company came backstage and said he'd like to make a test. He said, "I think you ought to do all right in pictures."

I'm as funny as the situation is, if I don't dramatize it. I *think* funny. I don't like broad comedy, the force comic who wants to push it down your throat. I like the Stan Laurel type — you don't do anything, but what you do is funny. In one picture, I split my pants. They made a shot 300 feet long, of me sewing a patch on my ass.

Everybody was chasing Chaplin. You hadn't a chance. That guy was way out in front. I met Charlie many times; we got along pretty well in the early days. But then he moved up in class. I don't think he behaved differently; he'd moved up. He deserved it.

I dropped two-reelers, then Hal Roach approached me to make some more. I [asked] Stan Laurel to direct. We used to kill ourselves laughing. In one picture I had to get rid of a body so I put it on my back and took it out in the country some place. We started to think about it and I said, "What do we do with the body?" And that became a gag with us. When we were stuck for a gag we'd ask ourselves, "What do we do with the body?"

I made two or three with Stan; I had Babe Hardy as my heavy in them. Then I said, "These things are passé." I could tell by the audience reaction; they weren't going over. I thought two-reelers were dead. I had to get moving, and feature films were the next field.

I've worked with some of the best people in the business. They'd bring me in just to liven up part of a scene — comic relief, they used to call it. I was high up in the saddle in the early days, doing this comedy relief stuff. You made a good deal of money on it, and you knew how much you were going to get; you knew by reading the script where you were likely to be, and you were ahead of the mark.

George Bancroft and I were shipmates in *The Docks of New York*, stoking the coal in the oven. They brought over this German director, Josef von Sternberg. In one scene we had to go down a rope ladder; they're the most difficult things, if you don't know how to use them. Sternberg complained that I didn't get down fast enough.

He said, "I'll show you how to do it." I said, "Go ahead." He bloody near fell. He got so wound up, he walked up to me and he said, "*You* British..." I popped him on the chin, and I walked off the set. I stayed home about a week. Then we finished it, but he turned it over to the assistant when they had to do a scene I was in.

I made a lot of pictures with John Ford. He'd try to get you mad. He used to swing at me; he'd come up to you and he'd go, "Boom!" And he'd clip you. One time I clipped him back. He said, "You stupid bastard. I'm playing with you." I said, "Well, play a little less."

I retired when I thought I'd had about enough of it. They were bringing in strong people, and I'd gotten myself up to a salary that was asking a hell of a lot from them, for what they would get. The last picture I did was *Donovan's Reef* with John Wayne. I don't think I had done anything in 14 or 15 years. Ford called and said, "I want you to do something for me." I said, "When?" "Tomorrow." That's the only picture — of all the bloody pictures I've done — that I get residuals from.

I used to visit Stan Laurel quite a lot in his later years. We used to sing the old music hall songs, and all this bloody stupid stuff. He'd say, "I've got another one for you" — and he'd remember this baggy pants comic who used to do the splits, and then pull his legs together by grabbing his pants in the middle. And we'd do the songs:

Once I thought I'd like to take a trip down by the sea.
I thought I'd like to bring a piece of seaweed home with me.
It tells you if it's going to rain or if it's going to snow;
It tells you quite a lot of things that you would like to know...

Clyde Cook died in his sleep on August 13, 1984, at the age of 92, at his home in Carpinteria, California.

Bibliography

EUBIE BLAKE

Kimball, Robert and Bolcom, William. *Reminiscing with Sissle and Blake,* New York: Viking Press, 1973.

Rose, Al. *Eubie Blake,* New York: Schirmer Books, 1979.

Young, Jordan R. "Eubie at 96," *The Los Angeles Herald Examiner,* January 28, 1980.

ELEANOR BOARDMAN

Ragan, David. *Who's Who in Hollywood 1900-1976,* New Rochelle, N.Y.: Arlington House, 1976.

Springer, John and Hamilton, Jack. *They Had Faces Then,* Secaucus, N.J.: Citadel Press, 1974.

CLYDE COOK

Lahue, Kalton C. and Gill, Sam. *Clown Princes and Court Jesters,* Cranbury, N.J.: A.S. Barnes, 1970.

Young, Jordan R. "Veteran of Silent Era Speaks Up," *The Los Angeles Times,* August 22, 1980.

MOUSIE GARNER

Young, Jordan R. "Mousie Garner: Chaotic Comic," *The Los Angeles Times,* July 11, 1980.

JESTER HAIRSTON

McLellan, Joseph. "From 'Bwana' to Chorister," *The Washington Post,* August 22, 1978.

Maxwell, Jessica. "Make a Joyful Noise," *California Magazine,* July 1979.

Pope, John. "The Jester," *The States-Item,* New Orleans, January 26. 1979.

Young, Jordan R. "Preserving the Spirituals," *The Los Angeles Times,* April 28, 1978.

HUNTZ HALL

Hayes, David and Walker, Brent. "The Films of the Bowery Boys," Secaucus, N.J.: Citadel Press, 1984.

Sherman, Sam. "Broadway to Bowery and Back," *Screen Thrills Illustrated,* July 1963.

Young, Jordan R. "Bowery Boys Films Were Not a Dead End For Actor Huntz Hall," *The Los Angeles Herald Examiner*, May 24, 1979.

RAY JOHNSON
"Spokane Boys Share Gershwin Success," *The Spokesman-Review*, Spokane, February 1, 1931.

MICKEY KATZ
Debenham, Warren. *Laughter on Record: A Comedy Discography*, Metuchen, N.J.: Scarecrow Press, 1988.

Epstein, Andrew. "The Mensch Named Mickey," *The Los Angeles Times*, September 30, 1979.

Katz, Mickey, as told to Coons, Hannibal. *Papa, Play for Me*, New York: Simon and Schuster, 1977.

Young, Jordan R. "Life Is Just a Bowl of Borscht," *The Los Angeles Times*, December 30, 1977.

LAURA LA PLANTE
"Laura La Plante," *Films in Review*, August 1980.

Young, Jordan R. "Laura La Plante: The Girl Next Door," *The Los Angeles Times*, December 27, 1980.

JACK LEMMON
Baltake, Joe. *Jack Lemmon: His Films and Career*, Secaucus, N.J.: Citadel Press, 1986.

Maynard, Richard. "Lemmon Live!" *Emmy*, July-August 1985.

Widener, Don. *Lemmon: A Biography*, New York: Macmillan, 1975.

Young, Jordan R. "Actor Jack Lemmon Does His Best When He's Afraid," *The Los Angeles Herald-Examiner*, September 18, 1978.

SPANKY McFARLAND
Hersh, Stuart. "Spanky McFarland — The Littlest Rascal," *VCR*, July 1986.

Maltin, Leonard and Bann, Richard W. *Our Gang: The Life and Times of the Little Rascals*, New York: Crown, 1977.

Young, Jordan R. "Our Gang Star Recalls Acting Days," *The Los Angeles Times*, 1981.

MARY MacLAREN

Hoaglin, Jess. "Stars of the Past," *Hollywood Independent,* January 1975.

Ragan, David. *Who's Who in Hollywood 1900-1976,* New Rochelle, N.Y.: Arlington House, 1976.

BILL McLINN

Franklin, Ben A. "The Candidate From Hannibal, Mo.," *The New York Times,* June 22, 1984.

Herrin, Angelia. "The Twain Campaign: Stumping for Everyone," *The Washington Post,* June 19, 1984.

MARCEL MARCEAU

Drake, Sylvie. "Marceau: Sculptor of Space," *The Los Angeles Times,* March 27, 1980.

Martin, Ben. *Marcel Marceau: Master of Mime,* London: Paddington Press, 1978.

Wong, Herman. "Quiet: Marceau Is Talking of Clowns," *The Los Angeles Times,* February 5, 1988.

Young, Jordan R. "I am a silent witness of my time," *The Christian Science Monitor,* February 2, 1977.

JACK NICHOLSON

"Star with the killer smile," *Time,* August 12, 1974.

Brode, Douglas. *The Films of Jack Nicholson,* Secaucus, N.J.: Citadel Press, 1987.

Crane, Robert D. and Fryer, Christopher. *Jack Nicholson: Face to Face,* M. Evans and Company, 1975.

Downing, David. *Jack Nicholson: A Biography.* New York: Stein and Day, 1984.

REGINALD OWEN

Parish, James R. and Bowers, Ronald L. *The MGM Stock Company: The Golden Era,* New Rochelle, N.Y.: Arlington House, 1973.

Rigdon, Walter, ed. *The Biographical Encyclopedia and Who's Who of the American Theatre,* New York: James Heineman, 1966.

DOROTHY REVIER

Springer, John and Hamilton, Jack. *They Had Faces Then,* Secaucus, N.J.: Citadel Press, 1974.

GEORGE ROCK

Price, Hardy. "Music Mix Same, Yet it's Rock," *Arizona Republic,* October 12, 1975.

Young, Jordan R. *Spike Jones and his City Slickers,* Beverly Hills: Moonstone Press, 1984.

PETER SELLERS

Evans, Peter. *Peter Sellers: The Mask Behind the Mask,* Englewood Cliffs, N.J.: Prentice-Hall, 1968.

Schickel, Richard. "Sellers Strikes Again," *Time,* March 3, 1980.

Sylvester, Derek. *Peter Sellers,* New York: Proteus, 1981.

Young, Jordan R. "Inspector Clouseau Strikes Again — And Again and Again," *The New York Times,* July 16, 1978.

RED SKELTON

Davidson, Bill. "I'm Nuts and I Know It," *The Saturday Evening Post,* June 17, 1967.

Maltin, Leonard. *The Great Movie Comedians,* New York: Crown, 1978.

Marx, Arthur. *Red Skelton,* New York: E.P. Dutton, 1979.

Young, Jordan R. "Red Skelton," *The Los Angeles Herald Examiner,* October 1, 1979.

DONALD SUTHERLAND

Craven, Jenny. *Films and Filming,* June 1979.

Flatley, Guy. "The Name Is Sutherland," *The New York Times,* February 15, 1970.

Martin, Sue and Mady-Kelly, Diana. "The people in Donald Sutherland's head," *Dramatics,* December 1987.

Young, Jordan R. "Sutherland: No More Goofy Roles," *The New York Times,* September 23, 1979.

DOODLES WEAVER

Page, Don. "Feetlebaum (Not Beetlebaum) Comeback," *The Los Angeles Herald Examiner,* June 16, 1974.

Young, Jordan R. *Spike Jones and his City Slickers,* Beverly Hills: Moonstone Press, 1984.

The Film Encyclopedia by Ephraim Katz (New York: T.Y. Crowell, 1979) is recommended as a source for filmographies and other data.

Index

Also Available from Moonstone Press

LAUREL AND HARDY: THE MAGIC BEHIND THE MOVIES
By Randy Skretvedt. A behind-the-scenes documentary on the making of
their classic comedies; with exclusive interviews and rare photographs.

REEL CHARACTERS: GREAT MOVIE CHARACTER ACTORS
By Jordan R. Young. Candid interviews with 12 of the movies' best loved
supporting players from Hollywood's Golden Era; with photographs.

SPIKE JONES AND HIS CITY SLICKERS
By Jordan R. Young. The unauthorized biography of the legendary
bandleader-comedian; with complete discography, interviews and rare
photographs.

Order Form

Please send the following books:

Qty   Amount

_____ *Let Me Entertain You* paperback @ $9.95   _____
_____ *Laurel and Hardy* paperback @ $14.95   _____
_____ *Laurel and Hardy* limited hardcover @ $24.95   _____
_____ *Reel Characters* paperback @ $9.95   _____
_____ *Reel Characters* limited hardcover @ $19.95   _____
_____ *Spike Jones* limited hardcover @ $19.95   _____
_____ *Spike Jones* paperback @ $14.95   _____

                                          Total for books   _____
         Postage: add $1.75 for first book, .50 each additional   _____
                         California residents please add 6% tax   _____
                              Amount enclosed (U.S. funds)   _____
Ship to:

IF THIS IS A LIBRARY COPY, PLEASE XEROX THIS PAGE.
SATISFACTION GUARANTEED OR PURCHASE PRICE REFUNDED.

MOONSTONE PRESS • P.O. Box 142 • Beverly Hills CA 90213